KOREA
1951–1953

by

John Miller, jr.
Owen J. Carroll, Major, U.S. Army
and
Margaret E. Tackley

MILITARY INSTRVCTION

Office of The Chief of Military History

DEPARTMENT OF THE ARMY

Library of Congress Catalog Card Number: 56–60005

For sale by the Superintendent of Documents, U.S. Government Printing Office
Washington, D.C. 20402

Foreword

In Korea the American soldier, with his Korean and United Nations allies, fought with bravery and skill against his communist foe and met the test in accordance with the best traditions of the service. His valor and determination defeated the communist aggression and stabilized the battle along the present demilitarized zone. The location of this line largely above the 38th parallel is historic evidence that in Korea aggression did not pay.

MAXWELL D. TAYLOR
General, United States Army
Chief of Staff

Preface

This volume records briefly, by text and photograph, the Korean conflict from January 1951 to the cessation of hostilities in July 1953. Like its predecessor, *Korea 1950,* it attempts to provide an accurate outline of events in order to show the U.S. Army veteran of the Korean conflict how the part he played was related to the larger plans and operations of the United Nations forces. For this reason *Korea 1951–1953* focuses on the operations of the United States Army but summarizes the achievements of the sister services and of the other United Nations troops in order to make clear the contributions of all to the successful resistance against armed aggression. It does not purport to be a final history. Fuller, more detailed histories of all phases of the Korean conflict are now being prepared by this Office. Two of these have already appeared in print: Captain Russell A. Gugeler's *Combat Actions in Korea* and Captain John G. Westover's *Combat Support in Korea,* both published by Combat Forces Press in Washington, D. C.

The text, which is based upon records and reports of the Far East Command, the United Nations Command, and the Eighth Army, was written by Dr. John Miller, jr., and Maj. Owen J. Carroll, using, in part, drafts prepared by Capt. Robert K. Sawyer and 1st Lt. Walter K. Lukens, Jr.

The photographic sections of this volume were prepared by Miss Margaret E. Tackley.

The maps appearing with the text were prepared under the supervision of Mr. Wsevolod Aglaimoff. Those inside the front and back covers are from Army Map Service.

A. C. SMITH
Major General, U.S. Army
Chief of Military History

Contents

1 JULY 1952–27 JULY 1953

Illustrations

Maps

1 JANUARY–21 APRIL 1951

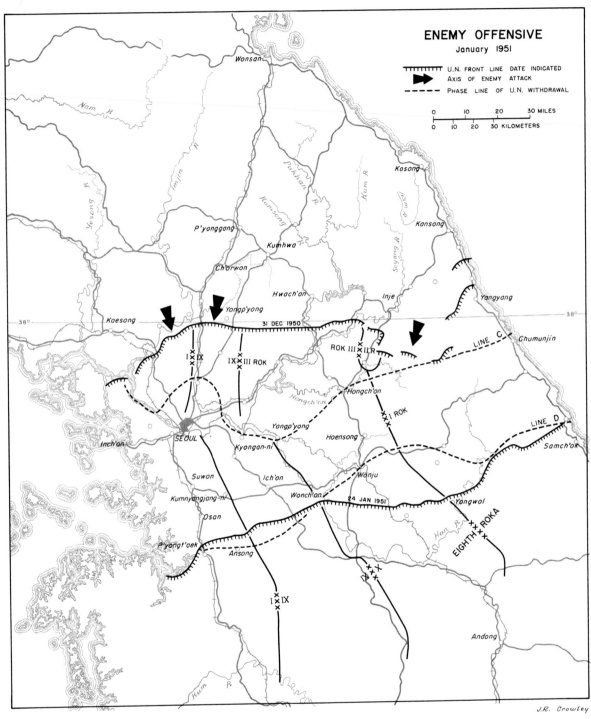

ENEMY OFFENSIVE
January 1951

	U.N. FRONT LINE DATE INDICATED
	AXIS OF ENEMY ATTACK
	PHASE LINE OF U.N. WITHDRAWAL

MAP 1

CHAPTER I

The Enemy High Tide

1–24 January 1951

As the first day of 1951 dawned in Korea, weary soldiers of the United Nations braced themselves to withstand the expected onslaught of North Korean and Chinese armies. The outlook for the United Nations, though not hopeless, was far from promising, for the unpredictable history of the fighting in Korea seemed only to be repeating itself. Since the initial North Korean invasion across the 38th parallel into the Republic of Korea on 25 June 1950, the months had been filled with bitter reverses, gallant defenses, spectacular advances, sudden blows, and more withdrawals for the U.N. forces.

When United States forces were ordered to Korea in July 1950, the enemy's advance had forced them to withdraw to a relatively small perimeter in the vicinity of Pusan at the southeast tip of the Korean peninsula. Here, as several of the United Nations other than the United States sent in reinforcements, the beleaguered troops made a gallant and successful stand throughout the latter part of the grim summer of 1950. Then, on 15 September, when General of the Army Douglas MacArthur's forces made their spectacular amphibious envelopment at Inch'on, on Korea's west coast about halfway between the 37th and 38th parallels, the tide of war turned

abruptly in favor of the United Nations. The South Korean capital city of Seoul was recaptured; the troops broke out of the Pusan perimeter. As the North Koreans fled northward, the U.N. forces crossed the 38th parallel in hot pursuit. They scored a series of victories until late November 1950, when they launched an offensive directed toward seizing the line of the Yalu River, the boundary between North Korea and Manchuria, and ending the conflict.

But now the tide of war changed once again. Some Chinese Communist "volunteer" troops had appeared at the front in October, and in late November more "volunteer" forces, crossing over from Manchuria, struck in strength. They halted the U.N. advance, then forced a withdrawal.

The two principal ground commands in Korea, the U.S. Eighth Army and the U.S. X Corps, had been physically separated from each other when the Chinese struck. The Eighth Army was in the western portion of the Korean peninsula, the X Corps in the east, with towering mountains between. Both had been operating directly under the United Nations Command in Tokyo, which was led by General MacArthur, who in turn received orders from President Truman and the U.S. Joint Chiefs of Staff in Washington acting as executive agents for the United Nations Security Council.

December 1950 was a period of withdrawal and reorganization. The Eighth Army and attached Republic of Korea (ROK) forces withdrew rapidly to the south with Chinese forces in pursuit. The X Corps, valiantly resisting the enemy in the bitter cold of the northeastern mountains, made its way to Hungnam on the northeast coast. From there U.N. naval forces took it safely off in one of the greatest sea evacuations in all history. The corps was brought to the vicinity of Pusan for reorganization.

Meanwhile, in mid-December, the U.N. commanders selected a defense line for the Eighth Army. Lying generally along the 38th parallel, it started from the flats of the Han River delta south of the parallel, ran northeastward along the Imjin River, then bent eastward through steep mountains to the Sea of Japan. By the end of 1950, enemy forces estimated at nearly half a million men were poised in the snow-covered mountains along the 38th parallel.

On 30 December, General MacArthur warned the U.S. Joint Chiefs of Staff that the Chinese Communist forces could, if they desired to make the effort, drive the United Nations forces out of Korea. The United States Government, though anxious to avoid a full-scale war in Korea, was also determined to resist the Chinese-North Korean aggressors. Therefore, MacArthur was ordered to defend his positions, to retire, if forced, through a series of defense lines as far as the old 1950 perimeter around Pusan, to inflict as much damage on the enemy as possible, and to maintain his units intact. Though no one wished to evacuate Korea, MacArthur was authorized to withdraw his troops to Japan if that

drastic measure proved necessary to avoid severe losses. At this time, his forces for Korean operations included the U.S. Eighth Army with attached troops from nine other United Nations, the Army of the Republic of Korea, the Far East Air Forces, and the Far East Naval Forces.

To Lt. Gen. Matthew B. Ridgway, who replaced the late Gen. Walton H. Walker as commander of the U.S. Eighth Army on 26 December, MacArthur passed on the orders to defend positions, inflict maximum damage on the enemy, and maintain major units intact. Within this framework he vested Ridgway with complete authority to plan and execute operations in Korea and ceased the close supervision he had formerly exercised over the Eighth Army and the X Corps. He assigned the X Corps to the Eighth Army so that for the first time since the X Corps landed at Inch'on the Eighth Army commander controlled all U.N. ground troops in Korea. By now fifteen of the United Nations—the United States, Great Britain, Australia, Canada, New Zealand, India, South Africa, France, Greece, the Netherlands, the Philippines, Thailand, Turkey, Belgium, and Sweden—had troops in Korea.

Ridgway commanded about 365,000 men. The largest single contingent was the Army of the Republic of Korea, which was under his control but not part of the Eighth Army. The next largest was the Eighth Army, to which certain U.S. Air Force, U.S. Marine Corps, and several United Nations units, including Koreans, were attached. The U.N. command estimated that about 486,000 enemy troops, or twenty-one Chinese and twelve North Korean divisions, were committed to the Korean front and that reserves totaling over one million men were stationed near the Yalu, in Manchuria, or on the way to Manchuria.

In establishing the defense line along the 38th parallel in late December, General Ridgway concentrated the bulk of his Eighth Army forces in the relatively flat central and west sectors because it was obvious that the enemy was concentrating strong forces above Seoul. Maj. Gen. Frank W. Milburn's I Corps held the left (west) sector south of the Imjin River; on the right (east) of the I Corps, Maj. Gen. John B. Coulter's IX Corps held the center.[1] Because it was believed that the mountainous land in the east could be more easily held than the western portion of the peninsula, a seventy-mile mountain front was first assigned to the weakened ROK II Corps and the newly committed, inexperienced ROK III Corps. Shortly afterward these were reinforced by the ROK I Corps with the crack ROK Capital Division. The U.S. X Corps, under Maj. Gen. Edward M. Almond, was reorganizing in the vicinity of Pusan. The 1st Marine Division, until recently a part of the X Corps, was held in army reserve.

At daybreak on 1 January 1951, after a night of incessant mortar and artillery bombardment all along the line, enemy soldiers struck southward through minefields and barbed wire in great force. They attacked along the entire front but directed their major effort against the U.S. I and IX Corps in the west and center. Seven Chinese Communist armies and two North Korean corps penetrated deeply toward Seoul and the rail and road center of Wonju, in the central sector.[2] The only units escaping the fury of the attack were the U.S. 25th Division and the Turkish Brigade on the extreme left and the ROK Capital Division on the east coast.

As the offensive gained momentum General Ridgway reluctantly ordered the U.N. forces to pull back to a line which ran along the south bank of the frozen Han River to Yangp'yong, thence to the Sea of Japan through Hong'chon and Chumunjin. This line included a crescent-shaped bridgehead around Seoul which was intended to delay the enemy armies and deny them the Han River bridges. Co-ordinating their move with the retiring ROK forces in the east, the I and IX Corps pulled back to the Seoul bridgehead line. The U.S. X Corps (the 2d and 7th Infantry Divisions) re-entered the fight on 2 January; next day it assumed control of three additional ROK divisions in a new corps zone on the central front between the U.S. IX and the ROK III Corps. U.N. forces now presented a stronger, more solid front than they had in the tragic month of November 1950 when the Chinese had struck the widely separated Eighth Army and X Corps.

With three enemy armies comprising a total of nine divisions astride the northern approaches to Seoul, and a division from each of two adjacent armies in position to exploit successes, the South Korean capital was imminently threatened. The enemy, evidently sure that he would not be seriously opposed, followed up successes much faster than before. And though the Eighth Army fought hard, it could not check the advance.

In the belief that standing in place would invite destruction, General Ridgway decided to withdraw instead of holding his present line. Withdrawal offered the chance to preserve the U.N. forces and to capitalize on the fact that the enemy's logistical capabilities did not match his tactical abilities.

[1] The I Corps consisted of the U.S. 25th Infantry Division, the Republic of Korea (ROK) 1st Infantry Division, the Turkish Brigade, the 29th British Infantry Brigade; the IX Corps included the U.S. 1st Cavalry and 24th Infantry Divisions, the ROK 6th Infantry Division, the 27th British Commonwealth Brigade, and the Greek and Philippine Battalions.

[2] A Chinese army is equivalent in strength to a U.S. corps.

This weakness had been noted in China when the Communists' attacks against the Nationalist forces had invariably slowed down, then stalled after the first blow, presumably while the attacking units were resupplied and reinforced. The Chinese attacks against the American forces in November had followed the same pattern. Lacking complete motorized transport, and using pack horses, ox carts, and human backs to bring up supply, the enemy had outrun his supply lines and was forced to pause above the 38th parallel before continuing the attack.

Ridgway's decision to roll with the punch accorded with MacArthur's orders to maintain his units intact and to achieve "maximum punishment, maximum delay." U.N. forces would damage the enemy as much as possible while withdrawing to carefully selected defensive positions. When the attack stalled, the U.N. troops could strike back before the enemy's supplies and reinforcements came up.

As the enemy intensified his attacks and began crossing the ice of the Han River both east and west of Seoul, it became clear that the capital city bridgehead could not be held. Ridgway ordered another withdrawal south to a line in the vicinity of the 37th parallel. This line ran from P'yongt'aek on the Seoul–Taejon highway east through Ansong, northeast to Wonju, thence in a curving, irregular fashion to the east coast town of Samch'ok. The U.S. I and IX Corps were first to occupy intermediate positions in front of Suwon, about sixteen miles south of Seoul, to cover the removal of great stocks of supplies. Movement to the new line began on 3 January, with bumper-to-bumper columns of vehicles jamming the roads.

With the advancing enemy hard on their heels, the U.N. troops had no time to save nearly 500,000 gallons of fuel and 23,000 gallons of napalm at Kimpo Airfield west of Seoul. These were burned in a great holocaust, as were barracks, hangars, and other military installations.

On 4 January South Korean government officials and the U.N. troops pulled out of Seoul as the points of enemy columns entered it from the north. Incendiaries set to work, and office buildings, hotels, and shacks burned. Smoke swirled through the streets as civilians who had waited until the end in the hope that the capital might be saved stumbled along in a haze of wind-whipped embers. When the civil police left, bands of looters ranged the city. All during the day columns of U.N. jeeps, trucks, staff cars, and soldiers poured south over two engineer bridges that spanned the Han. Refugees clogged the single footbridge that was spared them. That night huge clouds of black smoke billowed up into the bleak winter sky as Seoul changed hands for the third time in a little more than six months.

Once Seoul was evacuated, its port of Inch'on was abandoned. Port troops and thousands of civilians were brought safely out, their withdrawal covered by carrier-based U.S. Marine aircraft and by gunfire from U.S., Canadian, Australian, and Dutch warships. Docks, quays, and cranes were destroyed, all stores that could not be taken were burned, and the last two LST's were floated off the mud flats as Chinese troops swarmed into the port area.

Endless streams of refugees from Seoul and North Korea flooded the roads and railways leading south. Some of the refugees carried only small bundles, others dragged rude carts loaded with household possessions, and still others had only the clothes on their backs. Many died of exposure and starvation. Families became separated, as children wandered and their frantic parents sought them among the milling throngs. Crying babies were taken from the backs of their dead mothers. Many old people gave up hope and squatted beside the roads waiting for death. Civil assistance authorities did their best to help, and provided food, clothing, and shelter of a sort for a large number, but there were too many to care for them all and great numbers of innocent victims perished.

The shifting masses endangered military operations. Refugees had always presented a problem, but now the homeless wanderers trying to reach Pusan, which was already jammed, clogged vital highways and railroads. Finally control points were established at key road and rail junctions to channel the people into the southwest provinces.

At the front the U.S. I and IX Corps fell back to their intermediate positions on the P'yongt'aek–Samch'ok line after the supplies at Suwon had been removed and the airfield installations were burned. Osan, where the U.S. 24th Division had begun its heroic delaying action almost six months before, was abandoned. But now the Chinese attacks in the west tapered off; the enemy pushed light forces south of Seoul but did not follow up in force. As the U.N. units withdrew farther south, contact with the enemy diminished sharply. Consequently, on 7 January, even before the I and IX Corps had occupied their new positions, the U.S. 27th Infantry (the "Wolfhound" regiment) of the 25th Division, reinforced with field artillery, tanks, engineers, and two air force liaison parties, pushed north from P'yongt'aek toward Osan without finding an enemy soldier. A IX Corps patrol went as far as Ich'on, east of Suwon, and met only scattered enemy detachments. Local patrols along the western front made no contact.

But the central and eastern fronts saw heavy fighting. The North Korean *II Corps,* in late December, had driven through the eastern mountains to place large numbers of enemy soldiers behind U.N. lines, and as the January offensive continued enemy guerrilla activities in these sectors increased. Obviously, these were carefully timed to coincide with the attacks from the north. Elusive enemy groups disrupted communications and raided military installations.

During the first days of January the situation in the U.S. X Corps area in the center was obscure. Contact had been lost with the ROK 5th and 8th Divisions to the X Corps' right; the ROK 9th Division was badly disorganized, and the ROK 2d Division had virtually disintegrated. Thus there were only isolated pockets of South Korean troops between the X Corps and the ROK III Corps, and an estimated 18,000 enemy soldiers poured into the gap. To counter this threat General Ridgway formed a defensive line facing east and northeast on the X Corps' right flank, and another to block the enemy's movement to the south. But the enemy had already penetrated so deeply and in such force that it looked as if U.N. forces would be forced to withdraw still farther south.

Now that Seoul had fallen, many enemy units shifted eastward to concentrate on driving through the rough, mountainous land along the Hongch'on–Hoengsong–Wonju axis. Success in this area would place the enemy in position to attack southwestward behind the U.S. I and IX Corps. Further, this attack threatened the railroad and highway between Hongch'on and Pusan, the main U.N. north-south supply route. The capture of Wonju, moreover, would seriously limit U.N. movement in central Korea. Thus when Hongch'on and Hoengsong were abandoned and the U.S.

7

X Corps retired in co-ordination with the withdrawals of the I and IX Corps to the P'yongt'aek–Samch'ok line, the enemy quickly followed up with strong attacks against Wonju.

Wonju was defended by elements of the U.S. 2d Division. This unit had suffered severe losses when it screened the Eighth Army withdrawal in North Korea in late 1950. Now reconstituted and strengthened by the French and Dutch Battalions, the "Indianheads" showed their mettle by making a stand on high ground immediately south of Wonju and holding in the face of repeated assaults by at least two divisions. January produced some of the worst weather of the winter, and air support was seriously limited. On 10 January, for example, the Far East Air Force could fly no close-support sorties. On other days during this period F-80 and F-84 jets skimmed the tops of hills through snow flurries and clouds to give what support they could. Thus lacking complete air support, and fighting in temperatures as low as 25 degrees below zero, the men of the 2d Division hurled back all the enemy's assaults and counterattacked time and again through knee-deep snow. But this defense was not enough. The almost total disintegration of the line to the 2d Division's right forced abandonment of Wonju. During this action the division was commanded by Maj. Gen. Robert B. McClure to 13 January, thereafter by Maj. Gen. Clark L. Ruffner.

By 10 January large numbers of the enemy had flooded through the gap to the 2d Division's right and infiltrated the ROK III Corps, while enemy guerrillas harried the supply lines. To meet this threat Ridgway ordered Maj. Gen. Oliver P. Smith to move his 1st Marine Division from the vicinity of Masan on the south coast northward to prevent enemy penetration from north of the Andong–Yongdok road on the east and to protect the supply routes to the ROK units.

With the central and eastern sectors seriously threatened, the west was now comparatively quiet. Patrols of the U.S. I and IX Corps ranged north in attempts to make contact with the enemy. Air reconnaissance in front of the I Corps revealed a build-up of enemy troops and supplies between Suwon and Osan, astride the main highway from Seoul to Taejon and Taegu. This, coupled with police reports of large groups of guerrillas between Taejon and Yongdong, indicated that the enemy might soon renew his attack along this main route to southeast Korea. But ground sightings and contacts in the I Corps sector were so few that it seemed the enemy was moving at night and avoiding roads, or that the bulk of his forces was moving eastward.

Clearly, General Ridgway needed more exact information about the enemy. To attempt to re-establish contact in the west, and to force the diversion of some forces from the X Corps sector, he planned Operation WOLFHOUND, a reconnaissance in force in the I Corps sector. Accordingly, the 27th Infantry was again reinforced with field artillery, tanks, and engineers and ordered north.

The task force struck out northward in the early morning hours of 15 January. A battalion from the U.S. 3d Infantry Division covered its right flank, while other units to the west delivered local covering attacks. Blown bridges and other obstacles that the withdrawing U.N. troops had set up were the chief impediments to the advance. As the task force moved north along the Seoul highway toward Osan, it passed over bare, frozen hills and through deserted villages where an occasional solitary civilian might be seen dimly beside his ruined home. Thin wisps of smoke showed the presence of other human beings in this barren land, but investigating patrols found only more wretched South Koreans huddling around small fires. Not a single enemy soldier was encountered until the task force reached a point just south of Osan, where it met and exchanged shots with a small enemy detachment, which then fled.

Advancing in two columns, the task force converged on Suwon the next day, 16 January, and met machine gun fire about 800 yards south of the ancient city. But by now the high command was satisfied, and ordered the task force to withdraw about twelve miles southward.

The Chief of Staff of the U.S. Army, General J. Lawton Collins, arrived in Korea in mid-January to assay the fighting qualities of the U.N. forces and promptly settled the question of evacuation. "As of now," he announced to news correspondents, "we are going to stay and fight." General Ridgway expressed his confidence in his troops, avowing that the Eighth Army could readily take care of itself in its present situation. The Eighth Army, Collins informed Washington on 17 January, was in good shape and constantly improving under Ridgway's leadership.

This optimism was confirmed by events to the east of the I and IX Corps. On 15 January, when the WOLFHOUND force moved north, U.N. troops south of Wonju had begun further withdrawals to a shorter defense line which ran roughly between Wonch'on and Yongwol. The situation in the central and eastern sectors, though still serious, had improved by the third week of the new year, and enemy pressure was gradually decreasing. Guerrillas still harassed the rear areas, but the threat was abating as U.N. troops contained and hunted down enemy irregulars. The enemy armies had suffered heavily in their efforts to drive down the center of the peninsula. In one action, for example, the North Korean *2d, 9th,* and *31st Divisions,* while trying to encircle the U.S. 2d Division, were estimated to have lost one thousand men per day to U.N. infantry, armor, artillery, and aircraft. Eighth Army headquarters later estimated that the hostile armies had lost 38,000 men during the first twenty-six days in January.

Broad expanses of the Eighth Army front had now become quiet, but quietness did not necessarily indicate that the enemy had given up his attempts to drive to Pusan. Air reconnaissance revealed that he was building up reserves or supplies and bringing up thousands of replacements to his depleted units. It became apparent that, as the U.N. troops developed their positions along the P'yongt'aek–Samch'ok line, the enemy thinned his forward elements, establishing screening forces to maintain light contact, and concentrated the bulk of his troops farther north.

General Ridgway, on 20 January, issued orders designed to exploit this situation. He directed his subordinate commanders to create opportunities for brief but violent counteraction with armor, artillery, infantry, and air power with the intention of disrupting enemy preparations for a new offensive. He found the moment promising. "Never have members of a military command," he told his troops, "had a greater challenge than we, or a finer opportunity to show ourselves and our people at their best—and thus be an honor to the profession of arms, and a credit to those who bred us."

As local patrols were still making very little contact, the U.S. IX Corps planned a reconnaissance in force on its front. For this mission a task force was organized out of elements of the 1st Cavalry Division, a Regular division which fought as infantry in World War II and in Korea. The force included the 3d Battalion, 8th Cavalry, the 70th Tank Battalion, a battery of field artillery, and a platoon of engineers. With the mission of conducting aggressive operations in a triangular area bounded by the towns of Kumnyangjang-ni, Ich'on, and Kyongan-ni, the force struck out at 0530, 22 January, and advanced northward to a point on the Ich'on–Kumnyangjang-ni road about five miles east of the latter town. There it split into two groups. One turned to the east and traveled as far as Och'on-ni without encountering any opposition. The other went west for nearly a mile, came under fire from a small enemy group which dispersed under an air strike, and then moved north for several thousand yards. This element encountered no more resistance until en route back to the U.N. lines, when it met and scattered another small hostile band.

This reconnaissance, and Operation WOLFHOUND, further demonstrated that the enemy did not occupy any positions close to the front lines of the U.S. I and IX Corps in strength. Therefore Ridgway scheduled a still larger operation, THUNDERBOLT, for 25 January. THUNDERBOLT was to be another reconnaissance in force, with each U.S. corps authorized to use one U.S. division and one ROK regiment. Since the terrain in the coastal sector was flatter and the road network denser, the I Corps planned to use five columns of infantry and armor, while the IX Corps employed but two. The operation was to be a methodical, co-ordinated advance designed to push through the area south of the Han River and seek out the enemy.

The two-day period preceding Operation THUNDERBOLT was unusually quiet, even in the zones of the U.S. X and ROK III Corps. The 1st Marine Division had the only contact with strong enemy forces—guerrillas to the south. Heavy snow impeded movement along the east coast, but active patrolling by ROK elements failed to locate any large enemy concentrations within fifteen miles of the front. In this setting, combat reconnaissance units of the I and IX Corps went forward on the night of 24 January to the line of departure for Operation THUNDERBOLT. The pendulum was swinging north again.

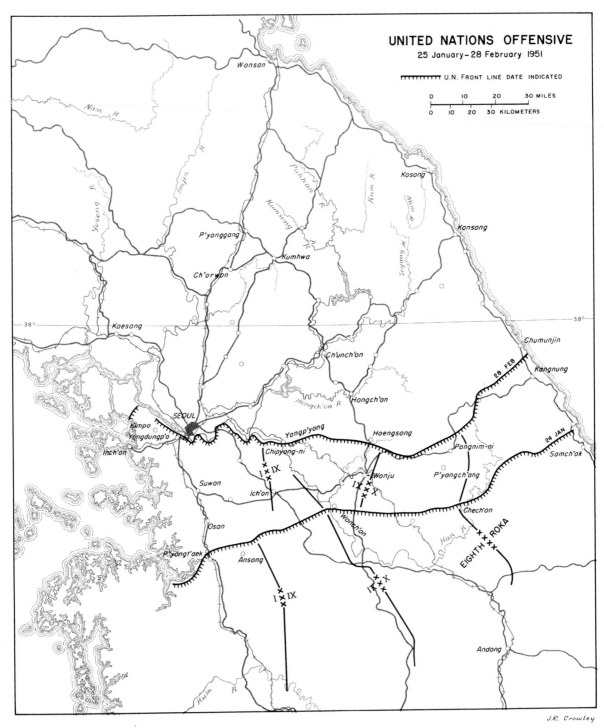

UNITED NATIONS OFFENSIVE
25 January – 28 February 1951

U.N. FRONT LINE DATE INDICATED

0   10   20   30 MILES
0   10   20   30 KILOMETERS

MAP 2

J.R. Crowley

CHAPTER II

Attack and Counterattack

25 January–28 February 1951

On the first day of THUNDERBOLT (25 January) six of the seven participating columns proceeded against scattered resistance. Only the Turkish Brigade east of Osan encountered stiff opposition. By nightfall elements of the U.S. 35th Infantry, 25th Division, were on the south edge of Suwon, and in the U.S. IX Corps zone a column reached Ich'on and took up positions north and east of the town. U.N. air units meanwhile co-ordinated their close support missions, armed reconnaissance, and interdictory attacks with the fire and movement of the advancing ground elements. General Ridgway requested U.N. naval forces to intensify their offshore patrolling along the west coast in order to prevent any amphibious infiltration of the army's left flank.

The support furnished by the air forces was most effective during this period. When Eighth Army foot elements flushed elusive enemy soldiers into the open, U.N. aircraft closed in to destroy them. Air strikes softened up points of resistance almost as fast as they developed. Most important was the damage being inflicted upon Communist supply lines by air power, which, according to air intelligence estimates, kept as much as 80 percent of the enemy's supplies from reaching his front lines. The enemy now

had to move not only ammunition but food down from the north, for local rice stockpiles had been removed or destroyed by withdrawing U.N. forces or burned during the fighting, and he could no longer live off the countryside.

During the rest of the month the U.S. I and IX Corps advanced slowly as all units proceeded cautiously and methodically, ridge by ridge, phase line by phase line, to clear out every enemy soldier. U.N. task forces advanced a limited distance each day. The tanks, "quad .50's" (multiple antiaircraft machine guns mounted on half-tracks), and field artillery would cover a certain number of hills with fire; and the infantry, under this cover, would sweep the same ground clean. Each pocket of resistance was wiped out before the next co-ordinated advance was made. The Eighth Army commander insisted that U.N. forces maintain a solid front, for an attempt to advance only in roadbound columns would surely invite the enemy to drive down the ridgelines between roads to U.N. rear areas.

During the first days of THUNDERBOLT the enemy launched a few small night counterattacks, but in general fought only outpost actions. Prisoners of war reported that only two divisions of the Chinese Communist *50th Army* occupied a front of nearly thirty miles, a strong indication that it had a screening mission.

But by 30 January resistance had stiffened, and the enemy began launching counterattacks in battalion strength. Hostile machine gun, mortar, and artillery fire north and northwest of Suwon increased, and in some sectors Chinese, armed only with grenades and sticks of dynamite, attacked. But the enemy still fought a delaying action. The U.S. 3d Division had joined the battle on 27 January, and as the operation continued it developed from a reconnaissance in force to a full-scale attack. Eighth Army troops were not only finding and destroying the enemy but were taking ground and holding it.

Then came indications that the extended frontage of the Chinese Communist *50th Army* was being greatly reduced. Identified from west to east across both corps' zones were the *148th, 149th,* and *150th Divisions* of the Chinese Communist *50th Army,* the North Korean *8th Division* and the *112th, 113th,* and *114th Divisions* of the Chinese Communist *38th Army.* U.N. air observers warned of numerous freshly dug enemy foxholes along the Inch'on–Yongdungp'o highway, and on the last day of January the U.S. I Corps advanced less than one mile, with some units engaging in hand-to-hand fighting. Nevertheless, U.N. armored spearheads probed aggressively toward Seoul, their way paved by massed Eighth Army artillery, bombing and napalm attacks, and naval gunfire that included the 16-inch rifles of the U.S. battleship *Missouri.* During Operation THUNDERBOLT, the Eighth Army was for the first time able to bring the full weight of two major weapons—armor and artillery—to bear on the Chinese enemy. In return, the enemy increased the size and strength of his counterattacks. Columns of U.N. tanks and other vehicles found roads heavily mined, and defensive mortar and artillery fire dropped into U.N. lines with mounting intensity.

The enemy resisted vigorously until 9 February, then abruptly gave way. Patrols that penetrated to a point three miles east of Inch'on reported no enemy activity. Other patrols raced north through a heavy snow storm, past abandoned foxholes and frozen rice paddies, to the Han River without contact. Task forces from the U.S. 25th Division made an 11,000-yard advance the following day to secure Inch'on and Kimpo Airfield without firing a shot. By nightfall on 10 February, the U.S. I Corps closed up to the south bank of the Han River and U.N. troops looked across at the capital city.

Although no massive amphibious invasion had been necessary to recapture Inch'on, the U.N. demolitions during the January evacuation were so complete that the port looked as if it had suffered another such destructive operation. The city was three-quarters destroyed. Piers were smashed and battered; barbed wire entanglements and twisted metal blocked the streets; buildings were blackened and deserted. At Kimpo hundreds of charred 55-gallon gasoline drums, which withdrawing U.N. troops had set afire, still littered the bomb-pocked runways, and the hangars were now but gaunt skeletons.

On the central front, meanwhile, U.N. armored patrols reached Wonju, now deserted except for a few civilians. Since there was little activity in the center and east at the end of January, Ridgway ordered the U.S. X Corps to create diversionary efforts to the north. Elements of the corps accordingly pushed toward Hoengsong along the Wonju–Hoengsong road, and captured the town on 2 February against light resistance. But presence of the North Korean *II* and *V Corps* in the vicinity foreshadowed stiffer

14

opposition to a farther advance northward.

The time now seemed ripe for more ambitious efforts. Ridgway instructed the X Corps and the ROK III Corps to initiate an attack similar to that being so successfully carried out in the zones of the U.S. I and IX Corps. The plan called for the ROK 5th and 8th Divisions of the X Corps to spearhead enveloping attacks on Hongch'on in order to disrupt the regrouping of North Korean forces south of the town. At the same time ROK III Corps units would advance in the central-east zone to protect the X Corps' right flank.

This attack, called Operation ROUNDUP, began on 5 February, and all units moved forward without opposition on the first day. By nightfall on the sixth, however, the ROK 5th and 8th Divisions were both meeting resistance. The former, on the right, found the going particularly difficult northeast of Hoengsong. Moreover, ROK III Corps units to the east could not keep pace with the advances in the central zone, and by 8 February strong North Korean forces were hitting the right flank of the U.S. X Corps. The ROK 5th Division therefore took up blocking positions along the exposed flank, and the ROK 3d Division was given the mission of continuing the envelopment of Hongch'on from the east.

For several days pressure on the U.S. X Corps increased steadily and signs pointed to a large enemy build-up on its front. U.N. troops encountered mine fields and booby-trapped foxholes. Although the enemy was definitely on the defensive he began launching stronger counterattacks all along the line. In some cases the enemy seemed to be trying to entice U.N. troops into attacking. Air observers reported the presence of large enemy groups north of the boundary between IX and X Corps and of other groups moving south and east above Hoengsong. In addition, U.N. intelligence thought it probable that the enemy had shifted the bulk of his forces in the west to the west-central zone, and the threat of a counter-offensive there became more likely as U.S. I and IX Corps closed up to the Han River.

This threat materialized on the night of 11–12 February, when elements of the Chinese Communist *40th* and *66th Armies* and the North Korean *V Corps* struck violently in subzero weather against the ROK 3d, 5th, and 8th Divisions, north of Hoengsong. Signaling his attack with bugle calls, whistles, and the beating of drums, the enemy made immediate penetrations and forced the ROK divisions to withdraw rapidly. Large enemy groups moved southeast through the snow-clogged, ice-glazed mountains in the battle zone, and air observers reported numerous enemy road blocks behind U.N. lines. The three ROK divisions attempted to build a defensive line just north of Hoengsong, but the situation had already deteriorated to a point where an organized defense was impossible. Only remnants of the ROK 5th and 8th Divisions remained. One regiment of the ROK 3d Division north of Hoengsong was surrounded, U.N. units became disorganized and individuals streamed southward, fighting desperately to break through the road blocks. Hoengsong was abandoned on 13 February, as Eighth Army troops battled their way south toward Wonju.

At nightfall on the 13th, the enemy attacked in strength at Chip'yong-ni, on the left hinge of the U.S. X Corps zone northwest of Wonju. This tiny village, no more than a few thatch-roofed huts clustered in a valley surrounded by snow-covered rocky peaks, happened to be the junction of several roads, and as such was a keystone of the central zone. If it fell the entire Eighth Army front might be endangered. The 23d Infantry of the U.S. 2d Division and the French Battalion formed a defensive perimeter on a ring of low hills immediately around the town, and by mid-morning of the 14th they were surrounded by a force later estimated to have comprised three Chinese Communist divisions. For three days the stalwart U.N. troops fiercely defended the Chip'yong-ni road junction against repeated assaults as enemy fire poured in on them from the surrounding mountains.

U.N. air forces dropped food and ammunition to the beleaguered men and destroyed hundreds of enemy troops with strafing and napalm attacks. Even at night, aircraft were able to give a measure of support by using magnesium flares to illuminate the battlefield. American and French ground troops were fighting gallantly when an armored task force from U.S. 5th Cavalry Regiment ran the gantlet of enemy fire to join them. The following day when weary American and French soldiers climbed out of their foxholes they found that enemy pressure had melted away.

For its extreme bravery in this action the French Battalion, commanded by Lt. Col. Ralph Monclar, a Foreign Legion veteran who had given up his four-star rank of *Général de Corps d'Armée* to take a battalion to Korea, was awarded the American Distinguished Unit Citation as were also the U.S. 23d Infantry and attached troops. The defense of Chip'yong-ni proved to be the turning point in the enemy advance.

During the action at Chip'yong-ni, some twelve miles of front had lain totally undefended between Chip'yong-ni and a point southwest of Wonju. Two units of the U.S. IX Corps, the ROK 6th Division and the 27th Commonwealth Brigade, hurriedly moved to fill the gap. Although the time lag in getting them to their assigned sectors could have been exploited by the enemy, he apparently was more intent on driving on the road junctions at Chip'yong-ni and Wonju, and the IX Corps filled the hole before he could act.

While U.N. soldiers were thus bitterly defending in the central and central-west sectors, strong North Korean forces had attacked northeast of Wonju in an attempt presumably to recapture P'yongch'ang. This attempt was believed to be an effort secondary to the major thrust in the U.S. X Corps zone, but the North Koreans soon made a deep penetration east of Wonju and drove to within ten kilometers of Chech'on to expose the right flank of the X Corps once more. General Ridgway had to muster all his resources to contain the enemy salient. Elements of the U.S. 7th Division and remnants of the recently disorganized ROK 3d and 5th Divisions hastily formed a defensive line north of Chech'on. The situation was unstable for several days, but the enemy's southward surge near Chech'on was at least temporarily arrested.

At the same time the U.S. I and IX Corps were gradually taking all the ground up to the Han River in their zones to the west. Some I Corps units were in position along the south bank west of Seoul. Here the action was confined largely to patrolling and duels between U.N. tanks and enemy self-propelled guns located across the river. Several ROK patrols attempted to slip over to the north bank, but were driven back by artillery and mortar fire. The South Korean capital was reported to be bristling with enemy troops, and it was estimated that the Chinese Communist *50th Army*, numbering approximately 18,000 men, was in the city itself, while the North Korean *8th* and *47th Infantry* and *17th Mechanized Divisions*, totaling about 19,800 men, were in the vicinity.

The enemy still retained a sizable foothold south of the Han, generally between Seoul and Yangp'yong. Although he defended it resolutely, troops of both U.S. corps were steadily narrowing it down. On the night of 13–14 February, a powerful enemy counterattack from the bridgehead pushed between two U.N. units and plunged into I Corps rear areas toward Suwon. This counterattack, probably intended to divert attention from the enemy's main effort in the central regions, was quickly contained. During the next day, U.S. troops searched out the hostile force and, by actual count, killed 1,152 and took 353 prisoners. The remaining enemy troops fled to the north.

Meanwhile, far to the south, guerrillas and remnants of the North Korean *II Corps* continued operations in the rear area. Although these forces were scattered throughout the entire southern Korean peninsula, large concentrations between Andong and Uisong posed a constant threat to the U.N. supply routes. No truck convoy was safe from the marauders. All attempts to destroy the guerrilla groups by attacks from a single direction had failed. The enemy simply fell back and disappeared. The U.S. 1st Marine Division, which fought them until the middle of February, soon learned the most effective technique: first, surround the hostile bands to prevent their escape; then, attack with the support of mortars and artillery.

Gradually the guerrillas became less active, less eager to fight, and prone to disperse after short skirmishes. It was estimated that U.N. counteractions had reduced the strength of these forces to about 18,000 by the end of February, a decline of approximately 15 percent during the first two months of 1951.

The last two weeks of February, however, saw the enemy strengthen his forces considerably on the fluid central front. Elements of nine Chinese divisions had been identified in the enemy offensive in the central zones, as well as elements of the North Korean *II* and *V Corps,* with the North Korean *III Corps* attached. In addition, one more Chinese Communist army was known to be immediately available.

The enemy attack at Chip'yong-ni had followed the expected pattern. Within a week after the initial blow the offensive had slowed down, and the enemy thinned his lines in the west-central area and around Wonju. The penetration by North Korean troops in the east-central zone had continued to move toward Chech'on, but the momentum of the thrust abated and it degenerated into infiltration. Two factors had apparently forced the enemy to suspend his offensive: tremendous casualties and the need to pause for resupply and reorganization.

When the Chinese Communists attacked in November, they had been fresh, confident, and unhurt. By the time their mid--February attack died down, they had been weakened by U.N. air and ground action, and had suffered cold, hunger, and disease. The cold, in particular, had affected the Chinese much more than the U.N. forces for most of them were inadequately clothed. Moreover, they did not have, by Western standards, proper medical facilities. As few towns were left standing, they could not find buildings to protect them from the freezing weather. When they did, U.N. aircraft wiped out the buildings along with the enemy soldiers. Frostbite and trench foot were taking their toll within enemy ranks and, if prisoners of war were to be believed, they were plagued by typhus, that age-old scourge of armies. Fighting 260 miles south of the Manchurian border, the Chinese found the situation quite different from that in November when they had had their bases to their immediate rear.

At 0745 on 18 February, Maj. Gen. Bryant E. Moore, who had assumed command of the U.S. IX Corps on 31 January, reported to Ridgway that one of the regiments in the sector of the U.S. 24th Division had found no opposition before it. The enemy's foxholes were empty, and abandoned weapons and cooking equipment lay strewn about. Eighth Army headquarters passed this information to the U.S. I and X Corps with the request that combat patrols be sent out to gain contact. The army commander warned that any withdrawal by the enemy might be a ruse, but findings of the patrols confirmed the fact that enemy forces along the entire Eighth Army central front were beginning a general retreat. General Ridgway immediately ordered U.S. X Corps to attack eastward to destroy the North Koreans on its eastern flank, near Chech'on. At the same time, he directed the IX Corps to seize positions running from Hajin to Yangp'yong, and thence northwest to the intersection of the U.S. IX Corps boundary with the Han River. These moves met very light, scattered resistance and disclosed evidence of hasty retreat. By 19 February the initiative all along the front had passed from the enemy into U.N. hands.

General Ridgway was determined to give the North Koreans and Chinese neither rest nor opportunity to reorganize. On 21 February, he inaugurated a general advance (Operation KILLER) by both the U.S. IX and X Corps to deny important positions to the enemy and to destroy as many hostile troops as could be found. The objective was a line which ran generally eastward from Yangp'yong on the Han River east of Seoul to points north of Chip'yong-ni and Hwangsong-ni, and thence eastward so as to secure the east-west portion of the Wonju–Kangnung road between Wonju and Pangnimni. In order to include the U.S. 1st Marine Division in KILLER, the boundary between the two corps was shifted eastward so that Wonju and Hoengsong fell within the IX Corps zone. The Marine division was relieved of its antiguerrilla mission and committed near Wonju as part of the IX Corps.

During the first week of Operation KILLER the U.N. troops advanced up to ten miles in the Chip'yong-ni area, and by 24 February the 1st Marine Division had seized the high ground overlooking Hoengsong. That same day General Moore, the U.S. IX Corps commander, died of a heart attack following a helicopter accident in which he and his pilot crashed into the Han River. General Smith, commander of the U.S. 1st Marine Division, assumed temporary command of the corps pending the arrival of Maj. Gen. William M. Hoge who took command on 5 March.

Advances in both corps zones were slow and unspectacular, for South Korea was just beginning to thaw. Swollen streams and mud greatly hampered military operations. In the X Corps zone thaws coupled with extremely mountainous terrain made each day's advance a test of endurance for both men and equipment. Heavy rains turned frozen rice paddies into treacherous brown slime, and men stumbled and slithered in deep mud. At night, U.N. troops scraped through sodden sand and muck to hack out foxholes in the frozen ground beneath. Though opposition in front of the U.S. IX Corps was heavy, enemy tactics along the entire central and central-east fronts were much like those encountered by Operation THUNDERBOLT a month before. Enemy groups contested U.N. advances, but their mission was plainly one of delay.

As U.N. troops began moving back into the areas lately occupied by the enemy, they found evidence of the effectiveness of their attacks. The hills around Wonju and Chech'on were littered with enemy dead. Many more had been buried in shallow graves on the bleak mountain sides. Apparently the Chinese and North Korean invaders had been even more severely mauled than had been imagined. The Eighth Army Psychological Warfare Branch went into action, and shortly thereafter the Fifth Air Force began dropping leaflets to the retreating enemy with the terse invitation: "Count your men!"

In the I Corps zone the Han River became a formidable obstacle shortly after the beginning of the thaws. Behind this obstacle the Communist defense of Seoul and other areas on the north bank was apparently being conducted with a reduced number of troops. The port of Inch'on was again in limited use, but many weeks would pass before piers, cranes, tidal gates, and other port installations could be fully restored. Kimpo Airfield would not again be operational until May.

In eight days U.N. forces had advanced to their assigned objectives in the central and central-east zones. Operation KILLER was nearly completed. Its success had been due in large measure not only to continuous pressure against an enemy who appeared unable to launch a major counterattack unless granted time to organize, but also to the strict observance of the basic tactical doctrine of co-ordinated movement.

On 28 February, after weeks of ceaseless hammering by U.N. forces, the Communist foothold south of the Han River collapsed. By 1 March the entire Eighth Army front was relatively stable. For the first time, the U.N. line had no gaping holes, no soft spots, and no enemy salients threatening to tear it in two.

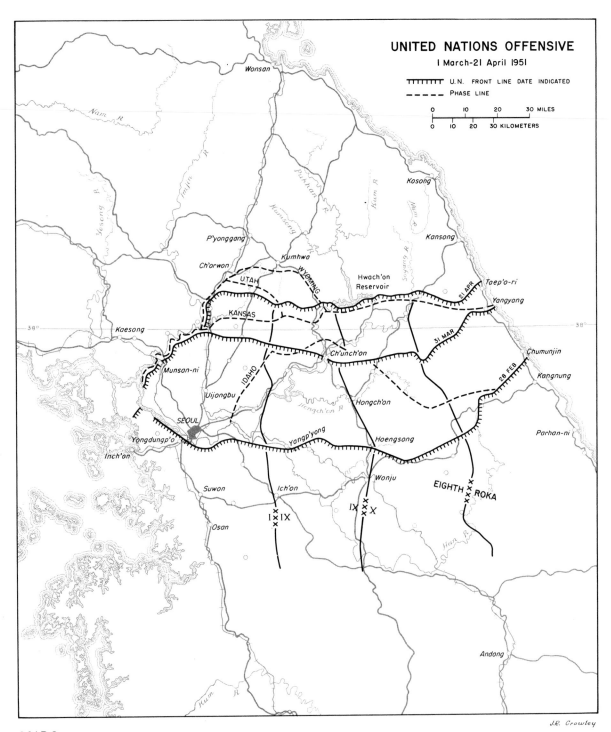

UNITED NATIONS OFFENSIVE
I March-21 April 1951

ⵊⵊⵊⵊⵊⵊ U.N. FRONT LINE DATE INDICATED

- - - - - PHASE LINE

MAP 3

CHAPTER III

Crossing the 38th Parallel

1 March–21 April 1951

Operation KILLER—the advance by the IX and X Corps—had not fulfilled all of General Ridgway's hopes for it, for the enemy had managed to withdraw while wretched weather was disrupting Allied road and rail movement. But in large part the recent losses had been recouped and the geographical objectives were attained by 1 March. The U.N. line, situated about halfway between the 37th and 38th parallels, swung in a concave arc from south of the Han River in the west through Yangp'yong and Hoengsong, then curved gently northeast to Kangnung.

With MacArthur's approval, Ridgway determined to continue the offensive with a new attack, Operation RIPPER. He planned to attack northward in the central and eastern zones to capture Hongch'on and Ch'unch'on and seize a line, designated IDAHO, just south of the 38th parallel. RIPPER's purpose was, again, to destroy enemy soldiers and equipment, to keep up pressure that would prevent the mounting of a counteroffensive, and to split the Chinese from the North Korean forces, most of which were posted on the eastern front. The U.S. IX and X Corps were to advance in the center through successive phase lines to IDAHO while the ROK units in the east covered the right flank with local attacks

and the I Corps in the west maintained its positions south and east of Seoul. The drive by the IX and X Corps would create a bulge east of the capital city from which U.N. forces could envelop it.

Operation RIPPER began on 7 March when, after one of the most tremendous artillery preparations of the war, the U.S. 25th Division crossed the Han River near its confluence with the Pukhan and established a bridgehead on the north bank. Simultaneously, the ROK 1st Division delivered a diversionary thrust northwest of Kimpo Airfield, and the U.S. 3d Division demonstrated along the Han River south of Seoul in an attempt to draw attention from the 25th Division. At first the enemy vigorously contested the bridgehead, but after three days of heavy fighting retired in disorder. In the central and eastern zones, U.N. forces made substantial gains on the first day, and thereafter moved steadily forward. Opposition to the drive took the form of a series of small unit delaying actions, a tactic well adapted to the rugged terrain. Wherever the land was least favorable to attacks, wherever roads were lacking, slopes precipitous, and natural approaches few, there the enemy held most stubbornly. For the next six weeks a grinding type of warfare prevailed. Nevertheless, by 11 March elements of the U.S. IX Corps had reached the first phase line. Other units reached it in the next two days, and the attack to the second phase line began on the 14th.

As intended by General Ridgway, the advance in the central and eastern zones had threatened the enemy's control of the capital. To search out the positions that still barred the way, a patrol from the ROK I Division crossed the Han River west of Seoul and proceeded northward for several miles before running into enemy fire. Another patrol probed the outer defenses of the city, found them almost deserted on the night of 14–15 March, and U.N. troops moved in. Thus Seoul changed hands for the fourth time. Within a matter of hours the Republic of Korea flag was raised over the National Assembly Building.

Heavily blasted by U.N. and enemy bombardment, some of its principal buildings the scenes of previous fighting, Seoul showed both new and old scars. The Bun Chon shopping district, untouched when U.N. troops had withdrawn in January, had been flattened. United States Ambassador John J. Muccio's official residence had taken two more direct hits. The great brass-studded red gates of the embassy compound were leveled and buried in rubble. No utilities were in operation. Streetcar and light wires dangled from poles. Of the city's original population of 1,500,000 only some 200,000 ragged civilians remained. By the end of March, however, a city government was once more functioning in Seoul.

During the next week the enemy fought only delaying actions. In the X Corps zone, some of the worst terrain yet encountered proved to be more of an obstacle than the enemy. The mountainous country consisted of high peaks and narrow valleys, and U.N. troops were constantly either descending sharp slopes or climbing steep heights to attack enemy positions that were sometimes above the clouds. Each enemy position was, in effect, a strong point which had to be approached, enveloped, and carried by assault. The early spring's rising temperatures were turning battlefields into quagmires. All supplies had to be hand-carried, and usually only the barest essentials reached the front lines. Prompt action by air rescue and evacuation units saved many wounded who otherwise would have died, for it sometimes took two days to carry the wounded out to litter jeeps. Far East Air Forces cargo aircraft contributed by dropping food and ammunition, and thus gave the ground forces greater flexibility. Despite the enemy and natural obstacles, Operation RIPPER ground slowly forward.

About this time Ridgway ordered the ROK I Corps in the east to complete the destruction of remnants of the North Korean *10th Division* in the Chungbong Mountains southwest of the coastal town of Parhan-ni. This enemy division, currently harassing the South Korean forces engaged in Operation RIPPER, had infiltrated southward in January through the mountains from the 38th parallel to within twenty miles of Taegu. Relying on the countryside for food and clothing and on captured matériel for ammunition, it had been able to make itself the full-time concern of at least one U.N. division plus ROK security forces. It had suffered constant attack and heavy losses. Because it had no medical facilities, only the fittest survived. Yet the North Korean *10th Division* managed to maintain the form of a military organization.

As early as 13 March, what was left of the division had made its way as far north as the Chungbong Mountains, where the surviving elements continued their operations. During the next few days, four ROK

22

regiments harried the North Koreans in an effort to wipe them out. Though the *10th Division* casualties were high, many must have survived to escape: the major activity in the sectors of the ROK 3d and 9th Divisions, on 17 and 18 March, consisted of fighting enemy groups that entered U.N. areas from the rear, fought their way through, and disappeared to the north.

With this threat eliminated, other ROK forces in the east were able to move to Line IDAHO by 17 March. The U.S. IX and X Corps neared their third phase line in the central zone and, Hongch'on having been secured, U.S. marines advanced toward Ch'unch'on. The enemy in this sector fought vigorously from bunkers which were little affected by aircraft and artillery attack. In many instances enemy soldiers had to be dislodged by the bayonet. Since Ch'unch'on was an enemy supply and communications center, and it seemed probable that the city could be taken only after a hard fight, the 187th Airborne Regimental Combat Team (RCT) was alerted to make a drop there on 22 March. By the 19th, when U.N. armored patrols entered the Ch'unch'on basin, it became apparent that the progress of Operation RIPPER and the withdrawal of the enemy had been so rapid that an airdrop would not be profitable. The project was canceled.

Once Seoul had fallen I Corps troops took up positions on a line from Yongdungp'o through the capital's northern suburbs, thence northeast. Ridgway then enlarged RIPPER to include a move by the I Corps westward to the Imjin River, and the corps began its attack on 22 March.

Next day the 187th Airborne RCT and two Ranger companies parachuted from more than 100 twin-tailed "Flying Boxcars" onto drop zones at Munsan-ni about 20 miles northwest of Seoul. An armored task force from the I Corps then rolled forward through mine fields and quickly made contact with the paratroopers. But the jump, which had been designed to block enemy movement along the Seoul–Kaesong axis and trap large numbers of enemy troops, failed to achieve these results. The enemy, here and elsewhere during Operation RIPPER, had elected to withdraw, rolling with the punch and trading space for time. His prompt withdrawal made the advance to the Imjin River rapid and very nearly bloodless.

This advance placed Eighth Army troops on the west flank of the enemy. The U.S. I Corps commander quickly ordered the 187th RCT to attack due east to capture the commanding ground behind the enemy troops facing the U.S. 3d Division. This move would allow the latter to attack and hammer the enemy against the anvil formed by the airborne regiment. But foul weather and all but impassable roads—supporting armored elements were forced to return to Seoul—slowed the eastward movement of the 187th RCT. By the time the objective was reached the enemy had withdrawn.

By the last days of March, as RIPPER came to a close, Ridgway's forces had fought their way through rain and mud generally to the 38th parallel. In the east the ROK III and I Corps had pushed patrols more than twelve miles north of the parallel, and by 31 March South Korean troops were in control of the roads leading west and south from Yangyang on the east coast. In the west, an American armored column probed over the line north of Uijongbu above Seoul. The enemy had pulled back and broken contact in many areas across the front. All U.N. forces were in position on Line IDAHO, and all geographical objectives had been taken. But the main body of the enemy had slipped away and escaped destruction. RIPPER was thus a qualified success.

Throughout February and March, U.N. naval forces played an important role in the Korean conflict. Ships from the navies of the United States, Australia, Canada, Great Britain, the Netherlands, New Zealand, the Republic of Korea, and Thailand constantly harassed the enemy. A blockading force had initiated a continuous bombardment of Wonsan and Songjin that was to surpass the Civil War record established when Federal ships shelled Vicksburg for forty-two consecutive days. Both Wonsan and Songjin were communications centers for the road and rail networks along the east coast, and the blockade and bombardment were designed to keep the supply arteries severed. By the end of March the siege was in its forty-third day.

In addition, South Korean units raided Wolsa Peninsula, about forty-five miles southwest of P'yongyang, killed and wounded a number of the garrison, and withdrew with a bag of prisoners. Similar raids were delivered at Inch'on, and ROK marines hit far up the east coast in the vicinity of Wonsan. The U.N. commanders launched these operations for several purposes: to inflict physical damage on the enemy; to net prisoners who could furnish valuable information; and to force the enemy to keep garrisons in areas where such raids might be expected.

When the main enemy forces had pulled back before RIPPER, it was to a line north of the 38th parallel which had apparently been built before the North Korean onslaught of June 1950. This line was probably the strongest position in enemy territory. The most stalwart portion of this line lay in the center, where a series of fortifications, built in solid rock and reinforced by logs and concrete, protected the road network and supply and assembly areas in the popularly termed "Iron Triangle" bounded by Ch'orwon, Kumhwa, and P'yonggang.

Sending U.N. troops in force across the 38th parallel was not an undertaking to be entered into lightly. A northward advance would lengthen their communication lines while correspondingly shortening the enemy's, and eventually a point would be reached where U.N. air superiority would be nullified. General MacArthur had reported that his forces could successfully proceed for one hundred miles over the parallel before they reached this point, but in the United States and among the other participating United Nations, it was all too easy to remember the debacle of late 1950 after the first U.N. crossing of the parallel. On the other hand, the enemy armies could not be allowed to regroup and reorganize unmolested for a counterattack which intelligence sources considered inevitable. To complicate matters, the forthcoming March–July rainy season would limit the mobility of armored and mechanized forces. The decision whether to cross the parallel or stand pat was a vital one. President Truman considered it a tactical decision which should be made by the responsible commander. The choice was made by Ridgway. With MacArthur's approval, he elected to continue the advance with the hope of achieving maximum destruction.

In making their plans, U.N. commanders were sure that the enemy was engaged in a full-scale buildup of troops and matériel not far to the north. While U.N. tactical advances were taking place, they gave careful consideration to the expected Chinese Communist spring offensive. That it would come was a foregone conclusion, and the only elements that remained in doubt were the time and the place of the attack. The enemy was still generally on the defensive, but there were definite offensive overtones in his actions. He was building no new positions farther to the rear. The Chinese were believed to have moved their *XIX Army Group* (consisting of the *63d, 64th,* and *65th Armies*) close to the Eighth Army's western front. If so, they could be expected to attack in the west and west-central zones over open, comparatively flat land, the only territory along the existing line where armor could be used advantageously. That armor would be used seemed certain, for air observers had reported the presence of the equivalent of one armored division and possibly two armored regiments in enemy rear areas. And on the central and central-east fronts, additional Chinese and North Korean troops had moved to within striking distance of the line.

By the end of the first week in April, U.N. intelligence officers reported that nine Chinese Communist armies had been positively identified, and ten more tentatively identified, together with eighteen North Korean divisions and six brigades. The combat efficiency of three of the armies had doubtless been reduced by the recent offensives, but the other armies were a formidable force.

The possibility that the enemy might use his increasing air strength—now believed to be a minimum of 750 aircraft of all types—was a cause for concern. Numerous reports and air photographs left little doubt that the North Koreans were making airfields ready for immediate use. In some instances runways were being lengthened to accommodate jets or bombers. In P'yongyang the enemy was readying a street to serve as a runway by demolishing adjacent houses. It was reasonable to assume that all this was intended to permit use of air power

in conjunction with a ground offensive.

In the face of these potential threats, it was better for the U.N. forces to move forward than to stand still. Thus on 5 April Ridgway followed RIPPER with Operation RUGGED, a general advance toward a new objective line called KANSAS. Running along commanding ground north of the 38th parallel, KANSAS was approximately 115 miles in length, including fourteen miles of tidal water on the left flank and, in the center, the ten-mile water barrier of the Hwach'on Reservoir, which was Seoul's source of water and electric power. The terrain on the right flank of this line was rough, nearly devoid of roads and therefore difficult for both U.N. and enemy units. But by shortening and strengthening their line, the U.N. commanders could use the water and terrain barriers to establish a stronger defense in depth. They could also make KANSAS the base for later operations designed to seize the Iron Triangle.

By 9 April, all units in the U.S. I and IX Corps and the ROK I Corps on the east coast had battled their way against fluctuating enemy resistance to positions on Line KANSAS. Although the U.S. X and ROK III Corps, in the central and central-east sectors, had been delayed by rugged terrain and hampered by the lack of adequate supply routes, they were steadily drawing up. On the same day, 9 April, the enemy opened several sluice gates of the dam that controlled the water passing from the Hwach'on Reservoir into the lower Pukhan River. The Pukhan, originating in the mountainous country to the north, flowed south to the reservoir and thence southwest to its confluence with the Han River east of Seoul. Within an hour the water level had risen several feet; one engineer bridge was broken, and IX Corps Engineers were forced to swing a second one back to the banks. To prevent the enemy from opening all eighteen sluice gates and flooding the Pukhan, a task force from the 7th Cavalry and the 4th Ranger Company was hastily organized and sent to seize the dam, close the gates, and immobilize the gate-opening machinery.

This raid failed for a variety of reasons: lack of enough landing craft, poor visibility, difficulty of movement over the almost trackless terrain, and stubborn enemy resistance. But the enemy's opening of the Hwach'on gates, while dramatic, had less effect on U.N. operations than originally feared and the task force was recalled after two days.

While the U.S. X and the ROK III Corps drew up to the KANSAS line, the U.S. I Corps and left-flank units of the IX Corps continued the advance by attacking toward Ch'orwon, the southwest corner of the Iron Triangle, with the intention of seizing a line designated UTAH which was in effect an outward bulge of KANSAS. As UTAH's northernmost point lay just south of Ch'orwon, this move would place the U.N. forces in position to strike at the Triangle. The main body of the IX Corps remained in position and patrolled, and on the east coast the ROK I Corps advanced by column of divisions.

During this period came a dramatic change in command. On 11 April, after a series of public utterances revealed sharp differences over national policy and military strategy, President Truman relieved General MacArthur of all his commands and replaced him with General Ridgway. Lt. Gen. James A. Van Fleet was dispatched posthaste from Washington to take command of the Eighth Army and attached forces. He arrived and assumed command on 14 April.

Meanwhile U.N. forces continued to edge forward, although the enemy burned off large areas of his front to create dense smoke screens that reduced the effectiveness of close air support. The Hwach'on Dam fell on 16 April, and on the east coast South Korean forces took Taep'o-ri. Other ROK troops north of Seoul sent patrols across the Imjin River and far to the northwest. By 17 April the Eighth Army's front-line units could not make contact with the enemy and U.S. IX Corps units not already moving joined in the advance north from Line KANSAS. Thereafter the general progress toward Line UTAH was virtually unopposed. Even as the advance continued, however, evidences of enemy preparation for counterattack continued to be reported to Van Fleet.

The enemy had long boasted in his press and radio releases that his offensive would be designed to force a military decision by either driving the U.N. forces from Korea or destroying them in the field. Van Fleet foresaw different results. His army had improved during the winter campaign. U.S. soldiers had become highly skilled in the months since they had entered the war as green occupation troops. Van Fleet decided to meet the expected attack by continuing the doctrines developed by his predecessor—those of "maximum punishment, maximum delay . . . ." The U.N. forces would, if compelled, buy time with space, and conduct a co-ordinated withdrawal to defensive positions well south of the 38th parallel, maintain contact with the enemy at all times, and inflict maximum losses on him by utilizing superior U.N. fire power from the ground and the air. When the offensive had run its course the Eighth Army would counterattack, cut the enemy's supply lines, and endeavor to destroy all hostile troops in the forward areas.

The U.N. campaign in Korea bore a striking resemblance to the Duke of Wellington's campaigns against Napoleon's armies in Spain and Portugal. Wellington, like U.N. commanders, was pitted against enemy forces that were capable of receiving steady overland reinforcements, while his troops, like those of the Eighth Army, were supplied chiefly by superior sea power. Wrote the Duke, describing his war of maneuver: "If they advance against me I shall retire before them, accepting battle if they give me a favorable opportunity, for the . . . action of my lines is superior to the shock action of their columns . . . ."

To anticipate an enemy offensive did not mean to sit and wait for it. By 19 April, all U.S. I and IX Corps units were in position along Line UTAH and preparing to continue the advance to Line WYOMING, an eastward extension of the UTAH bulge. After consolidating their gains for two days these corps started northward again. If this attack proved to be successful, U.N. forces would be on the high ground overlooking Ch'orwon at the base of the Iron Triangle. But during the daylight hours of 22 April enemy activity across the whole front sharply increased, and the U.N. offensive halted abruptly. Their lines alive with movement, the Chinese and North Koreans abandoned cover and concealment and moved boldly into the open. The expected enemy spring offensive was at hand.

SECTION 1

1–24 January 1951

CONGESTION ON THE HONGCH'ON–WONJU ROAD, central sector, 3 January 1951

33

AMMUNITION DUMP ON FIRE AT KIMPO AIRFIELD

BUILDINGS BURNING IN SEOUL as South Korean government officials and U.N. troops leave the city for the second time, 3 January.

35

TROOP–LOADED TANKS MOVIN

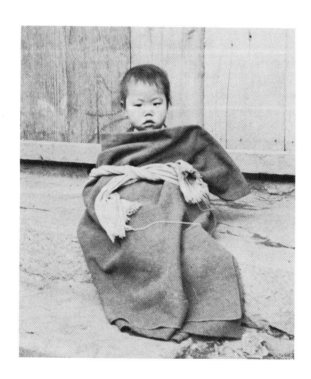

BABY–SAN WAITING FOR PARENTS to arrange passage out of Inch'on.

ᴏᴜᴛʜ after crossing the Han River.

Lᴀsᴛ Tʀᴏᴏᴘs Tᴏ Lᴇᴀᴠᴇ Iɴᴄʜ'ᴏɴ Hᴀʀʙᴏʀ boarding
an LST, 4 January.

RAIL BRIDGE ACROSS THE HAN RIVER is demolished by engineer troops. Both photographs were taken on 4 January.

PONTON BRIDGE SPANNING THE ICY HAN is blown up after last of the U.N. forces evacuate Seoul, 4 January.

Hordes of Refugees Fleeing from Seoul clogging a dike across rice paddies, 5 January.

A Seemingly Endless Column of South Koreans plodding

Two Korean Mothers pushing a cartload of their younger children.

through the heavy snow south of Kangnung near the east coast.

2D DIVISION VEHICLES IN MOUNTAIN PASS south of Wonju, 10 January. In this sector enemy troops flooded through the gap to the right of 2d Division positions and ROK III Corps lines.

SUPPLY CONVOY HELD UP by accident on icy highway. Temperatures reached 25 degrees below zero during the fighting for Wonju, attacked by Communist forces 7 January.

A 25-POUNDER FIELD GUN-HOWITZER. Artillerymen of the 29th British Brigade prepare to support the Turkish Brigade fighting in the west sector, 19 January. Both brigades were attached to the 25th Division.

ROK 3D DIVISION TROOPS ADVANCING to the mountains southeast of Yongwol on the central front, 20 January.

MOVING OUT over the frozen ground, X Corps area. Note rocket launcher in foreground.

25TH DIVISION TROOPS MOVING UP TO OSAN, 23 January. Operation THUNDERBOLT, a reconnaissance-in-force designed to seek out the enemy, was scheduled to start on 25 January.

GEN. J. LAWTON COLLINS, CHIEF OF STAFF, U.S. ARMY, stopping for a conference in Japan before going to Korea, is greeted by General of the Army Douglas MacArthur.

GEN. HOYT S. VANDENBERG, CHIEF OF STAFF, U.S. AIR FORCE (left), confers with Lt. Gen. George E. Stratemeyer, Commanding General, Far East Air Forces.

ARRIVING IN JAPAN after turning over their commands. Maj. Gen. David G. Barr (left) commanded the 7th Division and Maj. Gen. John H. Church the 24th Division.

GENERAL MACARTHUR VISITING NEAR THE FRONT LINES, north of Suwon, 28 January. He is accompanied by his military secretary, Maj. Gen. Courtney Whitney, 2d from left, and Lt. Gen. Matthew B. Ridgway, Commanding General, U.S. Eighth Army, wearing his characteristic grenade. Maj. Gen. William B. Kean, Commanding General, 25th Division, is behind General MacArthur.

"Hey, fellows! Look what Special Services gave us!"

"Western Jamboree," Special Services road show playing in the 25th Division area.

SECTION 2

25 January–28 February 1951

U.N. Aircraft Giving Close Support to the 1st Cavalry Division near Ich'on, 26 January.

96th Field Artillery Battalion Winding Its Way Through the Mountains to the 1st Cavalry Division area, 26 January.

Four Chinese Captured by ROK 1st Division north of Ansong.

Advancing West of Suwon on 27 January, U.N. troops pass a small village recently vacated by the Communist forces.

PREPARING BOXES OF C RATIONS TO BE AIRDROPPED

LAST-MINUTE INSPECTION OF CARGO BEFORE TAKING OFF

C-119 FLYING BOXCAR LOADED WITH CARGO flying

over jagged mountains to a drop zone, January 1951.

RECOVERING AN AIRDROPPED 55-GALLON
DRUM OF GASOLINE

KOREAN LABORERS ASSEMBLING AIRDROPPED
C RATIONS

58

"Talk about wires all fouled up—you know anyone at Fairfax 2-1991, Kansas City, Kansas?"

LINEMAN REPAIRING TELEPHONE LINES between Tanyang and Chech'on. Railroad is part of South Korea's main rail system from Pusan to Seoul.

Members of the 187th Airborne Regimental Combat Team firing the 75-mm. recoilless rifle, 5 February.

25th Division Men Observing White Phosphorus falling on enemy positions near the small village of Ansan.

5TH INFANTRYMEN PATROLLING IN RUGGED TERRAIN near the Han River, 5 February.

ASSISTANT SECRETARY OF THE ARMY EARL D. JOHNSON (center) with General Kean (left) and General Ridgway watching the 25th Division advance.

BACK FROM CAPTIVITY. Two American and four Australian soldiers in the 24th Division Medical Clearing Station after reaching U.S. lines.

15TH INFANTRYMEN fighting their way to the Han
River, 13 February.

CROSSROAD AT CHIP'YONG-NI, central Korean front. On 13 February the 23d Regimental Combat Team, 2d Division, and attached French Battalion were surrounded by three Chinese Communist divisions. For three days this U.N. force defended the road junction against assaults by the enemy entrenched in the surrounding mountains.

SUPPLIES COMING IN at the X Corps command post airstrip, Wonju, 12 February.

GREEK SOLDIERS SHARING THEIR WARMTH with an adopted Korean orphan.

AT CHIP'YONG-NI, 23 February. From left: General Ridgway; Maj. Gen. Charles D. Palmer, Commanding General, 1st Cavalry Division; Col. William A. Harris, Commanding Officer, 7th Cavalry Regiment; and Col. John Daskalopoules, Commanding Officer of Greek Battalion attached to the 7th Cavalry Regiment.

WALKING WOUNDED HEADING FOR AID STATIONS. Canadian infantryman is helped along by a fellow countryman, left; a 2d Division casualty is supported by an Australian soldier, right.

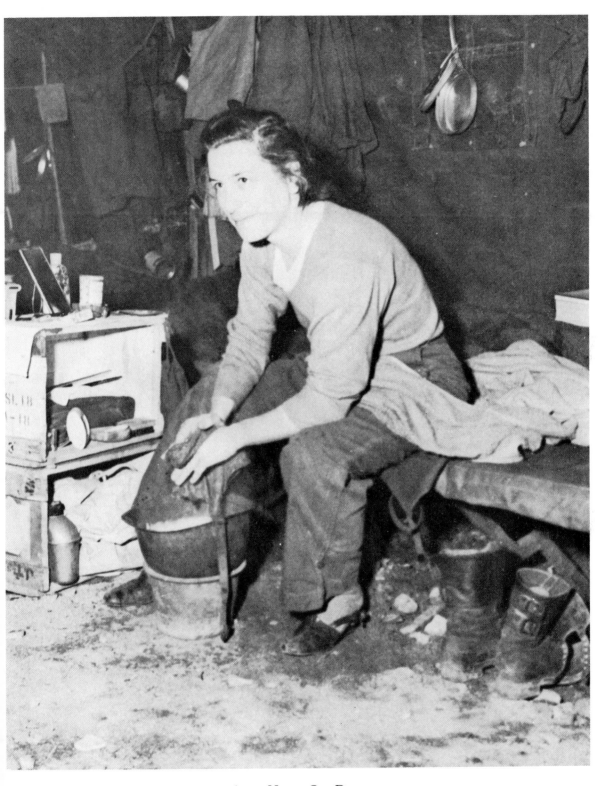

Army Nurse Off Duty

INFANTRYMEN OF THE 27TH REGIMENT CAUTIOUSLY MOVING UP A MOUNTAIN near Kyongan-ni, southeast of Seoul in the west sector, 17 February.

72

MEN OF THE 17TH INFANTRY TAKING COVER BEHIND A STONE WALL, 20 February. On 18 February the 17th Regimental Combat Team, 7th Division, attacked northwest from Chech'on in the central sector.

7TH DIVISION TROOPS TRUDGING UP HILL 675 after crossing the snow-covered valley (background). On 20 February Chuch'on-ni was secured.

ALL HANDS JOIN IN TO FIGHT A RAGING FIRE, 2d
Logistical Command, Pusan, 19 February.

74

CATCHING UP ON NEWS FROM HOME, 23 February. Men are from the Belgium–Luxembourg Battalion, which arrived in Korea on 31 January.

BRINGING IN ENEMY PRISONERS, 1st Cavalry Division area, 27 February. On 21 February Operation KILLER was launched along sixty miles of central Korean front to annihilate enemy forces and reestablish U.N. line east of Wonju.

SECTION 3

1 March–21 April 1951

White Phosphorus Shells Falling on Enemy Positions north of the Han. The 3d Division attempted to divert enemy attention from the 25th Division south of Seoul. Operation Ripper was launched on 7 March to take Ch'unch'on, an enemy supply and communications center, and outflank Seoul.

M4 TANKS OF THE 89TH TANK BATTALION, 25th Division, crossing the Han River near its confluence with the Pukhan River, 7 March.

COMPANY K, 32D REGIMENTAL COMBAT TEAM, NEARING THE TOP OF ANOTHER HILL. Smoke is from white phosphorus shells.

7TH DIVISION TROOPS moving north (above) rest their weary feet during a break along the road-side (below) near P'yongch'ang, east central sector.

Remains of a Hangar and Maintenance Shop

Seoul Two Days After It Was Retaken by U.N. Forces, 17 March.

AFTER CROSSING THE HONGCH'ON RIVER, men of the 5th Infantry tackle another enemy-held hill, central sector, 19 March.

ENEMY SOLDIERS BAGGED BY THE 5TH INFANTRY are escorted south, 24 March.

CROSSING AN ENEMY-MADE FOOTBRIDGE. The 24th Division advanced to positions northwest of Ch'ongp'yong-ni by 23 March.

187th Airborne Regimental Combat Team Practice-Jumping From C-119's, the twin-tailed "Flying Boxcars."

Preparing To Load for the Airdrop at Munsan-ni, designed to block enemy movement along the Seoul–Kaesong axis and trap large numbers of enemy troops, 23 March.

LOADED "FLYING BOXCARS" heading for the drop zone.

187TH IN POSITION EAST OF MUNSAN-NI. After parachuting in, the troops were ordered to capture the commanding heights behind the enemy troops facing the 3d Division.

3D DIVISION INFANTRYMEN CLIMBING UP THE TRAIL to their objective near Uijongbu, 23 March. By the end of the month the enemy had pulled back to a line north of the 38th parallel.

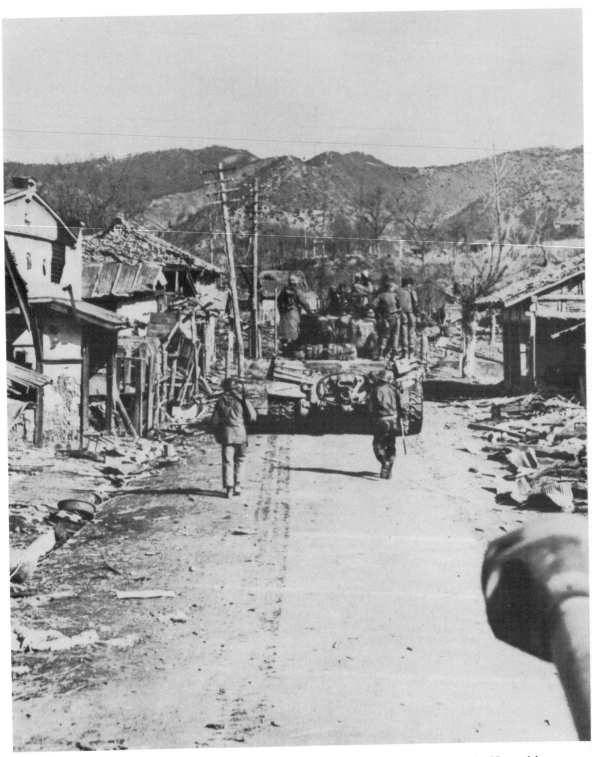

TANK-INFANTRY RECONNAISSANCE PATROL moving through a war-torn street in Hongch'on.

A BATTALION STAFF OF THE 1ST MARINE DIVISION observing artillery fire, central front, 17 March.

MEDIUM TANK M26 GRINDING ALONG A NARROW MOUNTAIN ROAD, central sector. On 23 March the 1st Marine Division advanced to positions north and east of Ch'unch'on.

CONVOY CROSSING THE SOYANG RIVER. By 8 April the 7th Division put two battalions across the Soyang River, and by 19 April U.N. forces were in position along Line UTAH.

MARSHALING YARD ON THE MAIN RAIL LINE leading south from Wonsan undergoing a fiery napalm bomb attack by B-26's of the 452d Light Bomb Wing, Fifth Air Force. Both Wonsan and Songjin were enemy communications centers for road and rail networks along the east coast of North Korea.

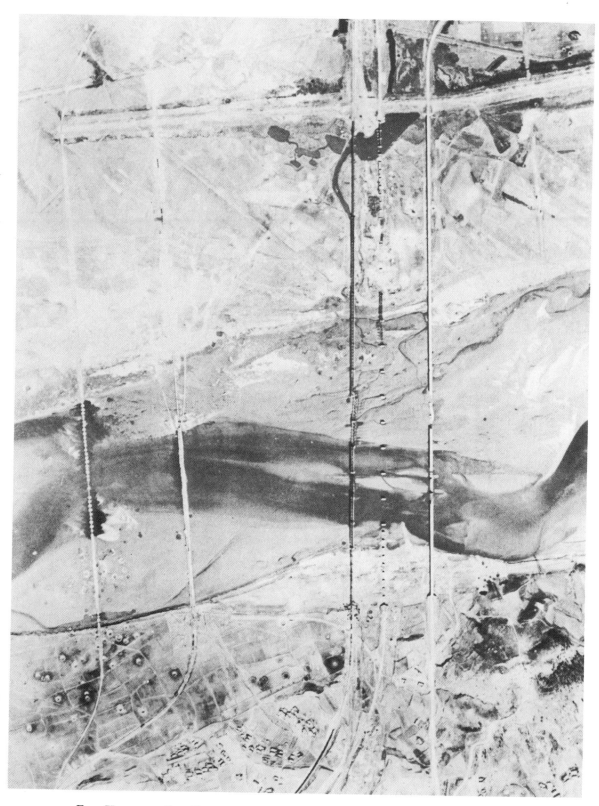

Five Knocked-Out Enemy Bridges over the Ch'ongch'on River near Sinanju.

Rolling Out the Red Carpet at Oakland, California, for the first marines rotated back home.

22 APRIL–12 NOVEMBER 1951

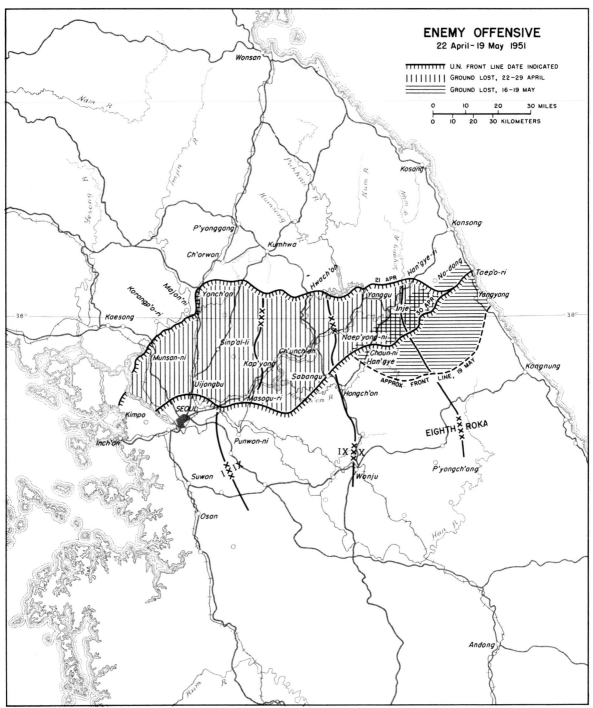

ENEMY OFFENSIVE
22 April-19 May 1951

| | | | | | | | | | U.N. FRONT LINE DATE INDICATED
| | | | | | | | | | GROUND LOST, 22-29 APRIL
GROUND LOST, 16-19 MAY

0   10   20   30 MILES
0   10   20   30 KILOMETERS

MAP 4

J.R. Crowley

CHAPTER IV

The Enemy Strikes Back

22 April–19 May 1951

By the light of a full moon in the early evening hours of 22 April, three Chinese Communist armies attacked the U.N. forces following four hours of artillery bombardment. The initial attack, a secondary one, was delivered through the Kwandok Mountains in the Yonch'on–Hwach'on area of central Korea. By daybreak the enemy was in motion across the whole peninsula.

Delivering his main effort against the U.S. I and IX Corps, the enemy attempted a double envelopment against the west sector to isolate Seoul, coupled with the secondary thrust in the Yonch'on–Hwach'on area and a push against the eastern part of the line near Inje. Radio P'yongyang announced that the ultimate objective—destruction of the U.N. command—would be readily accomplished. Of an estimated total of 700,000 available troops in Korea, the enemy commanders employed about half in the offensive, but they used little artillery, few tanks (contrary to U.N. expectations), and no close air support. Their tactics—assaults by a "human sea" of massed infantry—were the same as before, and again bugle calls and flares co-ordinated night attacks in which small units infiltrated the U.N. lines. When dawn came the enemy broke contact and, using camouflage and natural and man-made features, sought cover and concealment against artillery fire.

The U.N. lines held firm against the first assaults everywhere except in the central sector held by the IX Corps, where the ROK 6th Division was defending the center with the U.S. 24th Division on the left and the 1st Marine Division on the right. Here the enemy struck the ROK division in the Namdae River valley south of Kumhwa and drove it back. As the division withdrew in confusion south of the UTAH line, the enemy attempted to exploit his advantage by moving into the gap between the 24th Division and 1st Marine Division, which refused their exposed flanks and held on.

With his line cracked, General Van Fleet ordered the I and IX Corps to retire step by step to KANSAS while the infantry, supported by artillery and aircraft, slowed the enemy. Thus was lost the ground gained in the recent U.N. offensives. Task forces built around the U.S. 5th Cavalry and the 27th Commonwealth Brigade darted into the gap left by the ROK 6th Division, struck the advancing Chinese south of the 38th parallel, and stopped the exploitation. On the right the 1st Marine Division retired southward from the Hwach'on area to take up new positions before Ch'unch'on. When an enemy thrust cut the Seoul–Ch'unch'on–Kansong highway near Kap'yong on 26 April, Van Fleet pulled the IX Corps back to the Hongch'on River.

Meanwhile, although the enemy did not throw his full weight against Seoul until after the Seoul–Kansong road was cut, the I Corps was heavily engaged in the west. Fording the waist-deep Imjin River about midnight of 22 April, Chinese infantrymen established shallow bridgeheads on the south bank between Korangp'o-ri and Majon-ni. Other enemy troops cut south along the Ch'orwon–Seoul highway, but the I Corps slowed the attacking Chinese as it retired to the KANSAS line until the morning of 23 April, when the enemy drove the ROK 1st Division south of the KANSAS line. This setback exposed the left flank of the 1st Battalion, The Gloucestershire Regiment, of the British 29th Brigade. During the next few days this unit gallantly held its position even after it was isolated and virtually overrun. Only a handful of soldiers from the Gloucestershire battalion were able to make their way back to the main U.N. line.

Once the enemy had cut the Seoul–Kansong highway on 26 April, he put his weight into a strong attack against Seoul. Next day he outflanked Uijongbu and the U.S. 3d Division pulled back to positions four miles from the outskirts of Seoul while the ROK troops withdrew down the road from Munsan-ni. Van Fleet directed the establishment of a new transpeninsular line to halt the enemy in front of Seoul and north of the Han.

On 29 April U.N. pilots strafed an estimated 6,000 enemy soldiers when they tried to ferry the Han and attack down the Kimpo Peninsula to outflank Seoul from the west. The survivors were never able to offer a serious threat to the peninsula's defenders, the ROK 5th Marine Battalion.

The enemy also attempted to outflank Seoul to the east in the V-shaped area between the Han and the Pukhan Rivers, but the 24th and 25th Divisions checked this maneuver and held the enemy on the north bank of the Han in the vicinity of Kumgong'ni and Punwon-ni. On the east-central front North Koreans attacked the ROK units in the Yanggu–Inje area, made several gains, and captured Inje, but by 29 April their drive had been halted.

On this day General Van Fleet established a new line, not named and therefore termed NO-NAME-LINE which extended from north of Seoul to Sabangu, thence northeast across the 38th parallel to Taepori on the east coast. Because the major weight of the enemy's attack had struck in the west, Van Fleet reshuffled his units to put more American divisions there. Assigned to the I Corps, on the left, were the ROK 1st Division, and the U.S. 1st Cavalry and 25th Infantry Divisions, with the U.S. 3d Division in reserve. Holding the Kimpo Peninsula was the British 29th Brigade. The IX Corps, on the I Corps' right, had the 28th Commonwealth Brigade (this was the redesignated 27th Commonwealth Brigade), the U.S. 24th Division, the ROK 6th and 2d Divisions, and the U.S. 7th Division in line, with the U.S. 187th Airborne RCT in reserve. In the center the X Corps, consisting of the U.S. 1st Marine and 2d Infantry Divisions and the ROK 5th and 7th Divisions, held the line, and the ROK III and I Corps defended the eastern sector.

Thus by the end of April the U.N. infantrymen, strongly supported by artillery and air (U.N. airmen flew 7,420 sorties during the last eight days of the attack), had halted he enemy short of Seoul and the Han, and held a strong, continuous defense line. The enemy had fallen far short of his announced intention of destroying the U.N. forces. U.N. intelligence officers, reasoning on the basis of information gained by air reconnaissance, concluded that he would start another offensive soon.

While the Chinese and North Koreans regrouped and brought supplies forward, General Van Fleet decided to capitalize on the lull and take the initiative. During the first week of May regimental patrol bases were established almost eight miles in front of NO-NAME-LINE, and armored patrols ranged ten to twelve miles into enemy territory to harass the enemy troops that were withdrawing from NO-NAME-LINE. U.N. forces cleared the Kimpo Peninsula. The ROK 1st Division fought its way up the Munsan-ni road. Uijongbu fell to the 1st Cavalry Division on 6 May, and a 25th Division task force drove northeastward up the Seoul–Sinp'al-li highway. In the west-central sector an armored patrol regained control of the Seoul–Kap'yong road for the United Nations, and on 7 May U.S. marines dug North Koreans out of camouflaged bunkers on the Wonju road and captured Ch'unch'on. A task force consisting of the French Infantry Battalion, the U.S. 1st Ranger Company, one company of the U.S. 9th Infantry, and the U.S. 72d Tank Battalion probed northeast of Chaun-ni. On the extreme right the ROK III and I Corps also advanced northward. General Van Fleet then planned a general offensive based on NO-NAME-LINE designed to carry through to KANSAS, but increasing evidence that the enemy was preparing to resume the offensive forced the Eighth Army commander to postpone his plan.

The signs were unmistakable. After 10 May enemy resistance to local attacks stiffened. Airbase construction was still increasing. U.N. intelligence placed enemy air strength at 1,000 planes, with fifty new airbases being pushed to completion. Supply columns moving southward were reported daily, and air patrols noted heavy troop movements north of the IX Corps.

To cripple enemy air strength before the new offensive, the Fifth Air Force and the 1st Marine Aircraft Wing stepped up their attacks. A good example of their efforts came on 9 May when a total of 312 planes—F-80 Shooting Stars, F-84 Thunderjets, F-86 Sabres, F9F Panthers, F4U Corsairs, and F-51 Mustangs—struck at Sinuiju airbase on the south bank of the Yalu and reported demolishing fifteen enemy jets and over 100 buildings.

During the first ten days of May, when it looked as if the enemy would concentrate his attack west of the Pukhan River against Seoul, General Van Fleet had strengthened the western portion of his line. But between 10 and 15 May, according to intelligence reports, the Chinese had moved five armies eastward and deployed them in front of the Ch'unch'on–Inje area held by the U.S. X Corps and the ROK III Corps. Because time was short, Van Fleet decided not to shift his forces from the west, but he alerted the U.S. 3d Division, in I Corps reserve, to move out on his order. The rough and mountainous Ch'unch'on–Inje area generally favored the defender, but it would provide the attacker with some security from air and armor.

The daylight hours of 15 May saw all the usual signs of impending enemy attack, including an increased number of enemy agents trying to slip through the lines. Air patrols reported more bridge construction, and enemy probing attacks grew more numerous. Van Fleet's command made ready to stand firm.

By 14 May No-Name-Line had been considerably strengthened. The U.N. forces had laid mines, registered artillery, established bands of interlocking machine gun fire, and strung over 500 miles of barbed wire. Interspersed among the mine fields and barbed-wire networks were 55-gallon drums of gasoline and napalm, ready to be detonated electrically. General Van Fleet resolved not to yield ground, but to hold his line with all the weapons and power at his disposal. As he phrased it, "We must expend steel and fire, not men. . . . I want so many artillery holes that a man can step from one to the other."

After darkness fell on the night of 15–16 May, an estimated twenty-one Chinese divisions, flanked by three North Korean divisions in the west and six in the east, struck down the center of the peninsula against the U.S. X Corps and the ROK III Corps in the Naep'yong-ni–No-dong area. The X Corps held a thirty-seven-mile sector of No-Name-Line from the high ground west of Hongch'on northeastward to Inje. The U.S. 1st Marine Division held the left part of the corps line on the jagged terrain overlooking Ch'unch'on plain. To the right was the U.S. 2d Division, with the ROK 5th and 7th Divisions on its right, and the ROK III Corps to their right. Chinese units crossed the Pukhan River west of Ch'unch'on, and on 16 May other units struck hard against the ROK 5th and 7th Divisions. The patrol base regiments fell back to No-Name-Line, and by 1930 hours of 16 May the two ROK divisions were heavily engaged along a twenty-mile front in the vicinity of Han'gye-ri, a village ten miles northeast of Inje. The two divisions held their ground for a time, then fell back, disorganized and broken.

On the left (west) shoulder of the enemy salient, the U.S. 2d Division, including the French and Dutch Battalions, withstood resolute enemy attacks until 18 May, and then, together with the 1st Marine Division, moved right to fill the gap left by the two ROK divisions. The IX Corps extended its front to the right to cover the area left by the 2d Division and the marines. Van Fleet raced the 15th RCT of the U.S. 3d Division from Seoul to bolster the west face of the salient, and sent the 7th and 65th Infantry Regiments to blocking positions at the southernmost part of the penetration. The swarming columns of Chinese and North Koreans soon almost surrounded the 2d Division, pushing against its front, right, and rear. The Chinese even blocked the 2d's main supply route, but a co-ordinated attack by the U.S. 9th Infantry driving northward, and the U.S. 23d and 38th Infantry Regiments attacking southward along with their French and Dutch contingents, regained control of the route. The 2d Division stood fast and punished the enemy heavily. The 38th Field Artillery Battalion, firing in support, threw 12,000 105-mm rounds in twenty-four hours.

It was this kind of monumental artillery support which helped to create the so-called ammunition shortage that later was the subject of public debate and a Congressional investigation in the United States. All U.N. artillery units were firing the "Van Fleet load," which was five times larger than the ammunition allowance previously in use. The Van Fleet load, together with shortage of motor transport and the difficulties of supply inherent in mountain warfare, was largely responsible for the much publicized shortage.

Lt. Gen. Edward M. Almond, commanding the X Corps, ordered the 2d Division back to a new line south of Han'gye-ri on 18 May. The division, commanded by Maj. Gen. Clark L. Ruffner, successfully withdrew. During its defense it lost 900 men—killed, wounded, and missing—and estimated enemy casualties at 35,000. During this period, while the Seoul sector was relatively quiet, the divisions of the ROK III Corps, on the X Corps right, were heavily engaged, broke, and pulled back to the P'yongch'ang–Kangnung road. The ROK I Corps, on the coast, withdrew from Taep'o-ri to Kangnung.

While the battle raged on the central and eastern fronts, the enemy struck in the western sector held by Lt. Gen. Frank W. Milburn's I Corps and the IX Corps. On the night of 17 May, an enemy force estimated at 25,000 men struck down the Pukhan River toward the Han, but the U.S. 25th Division and the ROK 6th Division stopped this drive just south of Masogu-ri in three days of violent action. A weak attack directed against Seoul by some four North Korean battalions was quickly halted.

By 20 May the U.N. troops had brought the enemy's offensive to a standstill. The X Corps stabilized its front. The U.S. 1st Marine Division still held its portion of No-Name-Line, and the U.S. 2d Division, with the 15th Infantry attached, prepared to wrest the initiative from the Chinese and retake its positions on No-Name-Line. Having thus stopped two major enemy offensives in as many months, and with two more U.N. battalions about to join the Eighth Army, General Van Fleet decided to take the offensive again.

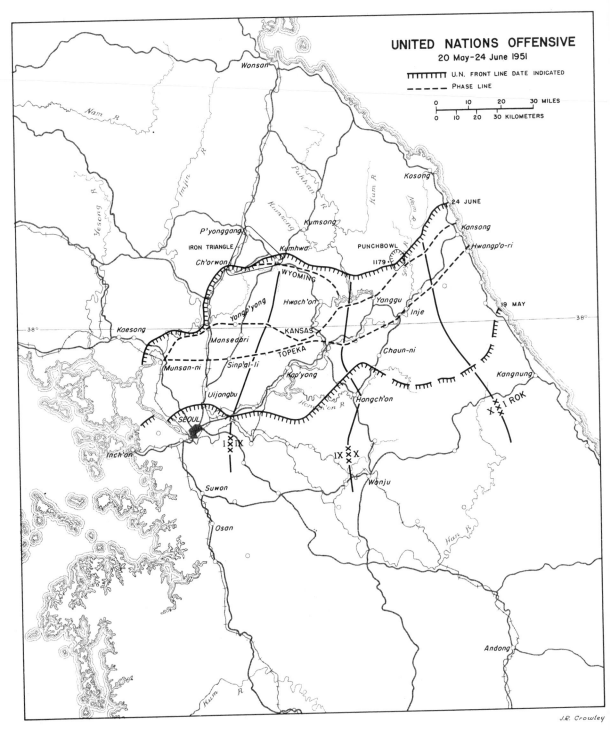

UNITED NATIONS OFFENSIVE
20 May-24 June 1951

U.N. FRONT LINE DATE INDICATED
PHASE LINE

MAP 5

CHAPTER V

The United Nations Resume the Advance

20 May–24 June 1951

General Van Fleet opened his new offensive with a series of local attacks designed to relieve enemy pressure on the U.S. X Corps. On 18 May he ordered the U.S. I and IX Corps, and the U.S. 1st Marine Division, the left flank element of the X Corps, to send out strong patrols and prepare to attack a phase line (TOPEKA) about halfway between NO-NAME-LINE and KANSAS. The next day, after bolstering the U.S. 3d Division by attaching to it the newly arrived Canadian 25th Brigade, he enlarged the goals of his offensive by directing the I, IX, and X Corps to advance to enemy supply and communications areas near Mansedari, Hwach'on, and Inje. The ROK I Corps, on the east, was to advance and conform to the movements of the X Corps' right flank. The ROK III Corps, which had recently broken under enemy attack, was deactivated. Together with part of the old ROK III Corps front, the ROK 9th Division was given to the X Corps, and the ROK 3d Division and its front were given to the ROK I Corps.

The new offensive, Van Fleet hoped, would deny the enemy any chance to gather himself for another counterstroke, threaten the enemy supply route in the Hwach'on Reservoir area, and eventually result in the capture of the Iron Triangle. He shifted boundaries to place the western third of the Hwach'on Reservoir in the IX Corps zone, leaving the remaining two thirds the responsibility of the X Corps. Once the X Corps had taken its objectives, he hoped to send it in an enveloping move northeastward to the coast to block the enemy while the ROK I Corps attacked northwestward. As he put it, "The 38th Parallel has no significance in the present tactical situation. . . . The Eighth Army will go wherever the situation dictates in hot pursuit of the enemy."

Once more, as the enemy pulled back, the United Nations forces rolled forward against generally light resistance. On 19 May units of the ROK 1st Division reconnoitered the Seoul highway toward Munsan-ni. Within the next few days I Corps troops reached the Imjin River north of Munsan-ni and entered Uijongbu and Sinp'al-li. Elements of the IX Corps pushed toward Kap'yong, drove the enemy across the Hongch'on River, and moved toward the Hwach'on Reservoir.

In the X Corps zone, while aircraft executed a continuous series of close support missions, the American divisions made ready to trap or destroy the enemy soldiers that had burst through the lines in the offensive just halted. Using tank-infantry task forces as well as regular formations, General Almond planned to employ the U.S. 1st Marine Division, on the left, in the Yanggu area to push the enemy back against the Hwach'on Reservoir while to the southeast the U.S. 3d Division struck at the farthest point of enemy penetration. At the same time, the 187th Airborne RCT was to drive northeast along the Hongch'on–Kansong highway to cut the enemy supply route at Inje, east of Yanggu, while a task force composed of American and Korean infantrymen covered the right flank. The ROK 8th and 9th Divisions were in reserve; the ROK 5th and 7th Divisions were reorganizing.

The 1st Marine Division attacked toward Yanggu at 0800 on 24 May, while the 187th RCT started out for Inje. One battalion of the airborne regiment broke loose and crossed the Soyang River the next day to hold a bridgehead pending the arrival of the 23d Infantry of the U.S. 2d Division two days later, when the 7th Marines also reached the Soyang. Almond formed a task force of the 187th, the U.S. 72d Tank Battalion, and other elements to drive to the coastal town of Kansong in accordance with Van Fleet's orders.

Although rain, mud, and enemy resistance slowed the offensive on 27 and 28 May, and in many instances permitted the enemy to withdraw with his supplies, the 187th had taken Inje by the 27th, the marines were making a final push toward the Hwach'on Reservoir and Yanggu, and the 17th Infantry of the 7th Division, in the IX Corps, had taken Hwach'on. At the end of the month the X Corps was deployed along the Soyang River. Its flanking drive to

Kansong proved unnecessary, for that town fell to the ROK Capital Division of the ROK I Corps.

The Eighth Army had scored a significant advance which had brought it just about back to the KANSAS line. The front now ran from Munsan-ni through Yong-p'yong, Hwach'on, and Yanggu, dipped southward sharply, and then swung north and east to Kansong. Except in the west where it slanted southward to take tactical advantage of the Imjin River, the line lay north of the 38th parallel. South Korea was virtually cleared of the enemy.

Enemy casualties for the last half of May, Eighth Army headquarters reported, included 17,000 counted dead and 17,000 prisoners of war. Its own casualties for the entire month numbered 33,770. The South Koreans had lost the most; American losses totaled 745 dead, 4,218 wounded, 572 missing, and 6,758 nonbattle casualties, most of which were caused by disease.

What should be done next? General Van Fleet's statement about the hot pursuit of the enemy did not mean that he intended another advance to the Yalu, for the Joint Chiefs of Staff had prescribed that the Eighth Army was not to go beyond the general vicinity of Line KANSAS. General Ridgway, however, had authorized local advances to gain better ground. In any event, it was clear that the U.N. forces were not numerous enough to encircle and destroy the enemy in large-scale maneuvers, but would have to stabilize along a strong defensive line. In addition to KANSAS, there were other transpeninsular lines—the Yesong River–Wonsan line, and the Sukch'on–Wonsan line north of the 39th parallel—that were relatively short; but they possessed less defensible terrain than KANSAS, their road systems were poorer, and to seize them would lengthen the U.N.

communications lines while shortening the enemy's. Clearly, then, the best policy appeared to be to defend KANSAS, meanwhile taking advantage of Ridgway's authorization to conduct local advances to more favorable ground.

On 1 June, therefore, Van Fleet directed reserve elements of his forces to clear out all civilians and to strengthen KANSAS by stringing barbed wire, clearing fields of fire, laying mines, constructing shelters with overhead cover, establishing trail and road blocks, and plotting artillery concentrations. He hoped thus to make the line virtually impregnable. Meanwhile the I and IX Corps were to continue their advance toward Line WYOMING, the bulge north of KANSAS that ran from the Imjin River to just south of Ch'orwon and Kumhwa, thence southeast. With this order Van Fleet lowered his sights slightly, for his earlier plans had aimed at capturing the Iron Triangle rather than stopping short on WYOMING.

This advance, dubbed Operation PILE-DRIVER, was carried out with comparative ease except along the approaches to the Iron Triangle where the enemy resisted stoutly. Except for a range of hills, the Triangle was a low-lying area surrounded by saw-toothed mountains. It was the terminus of a main highway from Manchuria and was interlaced with dirt roads and two single-track railroads. It served the enemy as a supply and communications area. Elements of both the I and IX Corps fought their way toward the WYOMING line near the Ch'orwon–Kumhwa base of the Triangle, and the enemy fought back hard from defenses arranged in depth. As happened so often, heavy rains in the first few days of June limited direct air support and turned the roads into veritable quagmires.

But the Eighth Army edged forward. The 1st Cavalry Division pushed from Uijongbu toward Ch'orwon against hard-fighting Chinese, as sweat-soaked engineer parties moved ahead of creeping tanks to probe for wooden box-mines. Infantrymen of the U.S. 3d and 25th Divisions used flame throwers against mud and log bunkers. By 10 June, aided by drier weather that made possible round-the-clock air support, the 3d Division, with the ROK 9th Division and the 10th Philippine Battalion, attacked and gained the high ground south of Ch'orwon, while the 25th Division and the Turkish Brigade fought their way to within three miles of Kumhwa. Next day at 1330 Ch'orwon fell, abandoned by the enemy; two hours later the Turkish Brigade entered Kumhwa, from which the enemy had also departed.

Now firmly in control of its portion of Line WYOMING, the I Corps sent out task forces to pursue the enemy. On 13 June two tank-infantry task forces, from Ch'orwon and Kumhwa, reached P'yonggang, which they found deserted. When they discovered that the enemy held the dominating ground north of the city, however, the two task forces quickly returned. Units of the IX Corps pushed northeast toward Kumsong and found the enemy present in strength and obviously establishing a defensive line. As the Triangle was dominated by the surrounding heights, neither side attempted to hold it in strength thereafter, although Chinese troops struck back at the I and IX Corps and reoccupied P'yonggang on 17 June.

On the east-central front, meanwhile, the X Corps had pushed through mountains toward its sector of the KANSAS line, which extended over a series of ridges from the Hwach'on Reservoir northeastward to the lower lip of the "Punchbowl," an aptly named circular depression north of Inje.

Using three divisions, the ROK 7th, the U.S. 1st Marine, and the ROK 5th (which had relieved the U.S. 2d Division), the X Corps ground forward against the North Korean *II* and *V Corps*. The enemy, well dug in on the ridge tops and amply supplied with machine guns, mortars, and artillery, fought back hard. Marines and South Koreans assaulted successive bunker-studded ridges to push the enemy out, and on 16 June elements of the 1st Marine Division reached KANSAS, while on the right of the X Corps the ROK I Corps advanced from Kansong toward Kosong.

Thus by mid-June the Eighth Army had largely attained the principal terrain objectives of PILEDRIVER, although the enemy had again managed to get away. Action for the rest of the month, except in the Punchbowl area where the 1st Marine Division fought a violent battle, was confined to developing the KANSAS and WYOMING lines, and to patrolling and local fights which, although fierce and bloody, did not materially affect the dispositions of either side.

As the first year of the Korean conflict came to an end, the United Nations could look back on their accomplishments with considerable satisfaction. South Korea had been cleared of the invading enemy, and the U.N. forces, after receiving and delivering severe batterings, had pushed north of the 38th parallel and successfully executed the missions that were within their power to accomplish. Thus, when on Sunday evening, 23 June, in New York City, Jacob Malik, Deputy Foreign Commissar of the Union of Soviet Socialist Republics and his country's delegate to the United Nations, proposed cease-fire discussions between the participants in the Korean conflict, his proposal, while it may have been made for the convenience of the Chinese, came at a fortunate time for the Eighth Army.

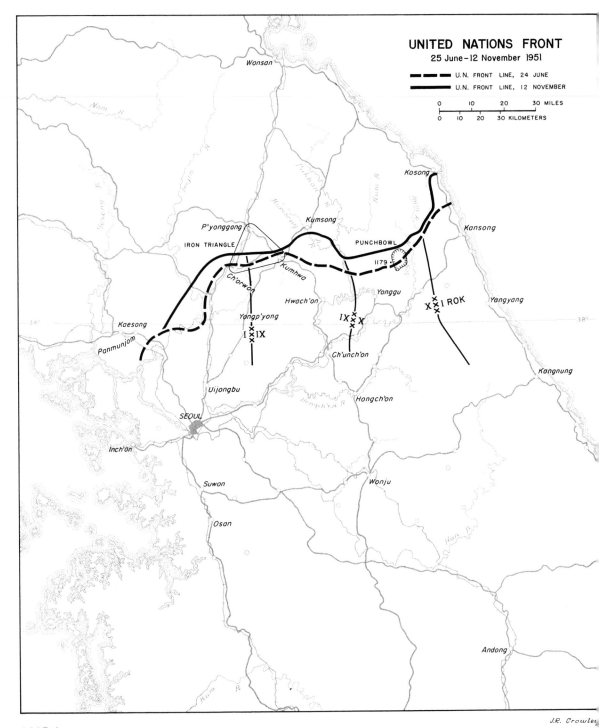

UNITED NATIONS FRONT
25 June-12 November 1951

U.N. FRONT LINE, 24 JUNE
U.N. FRONT LINE, 12 NOVEMBER

0   10   20   30 MILES
0   10   20   30 KILOMETERS

J.R. Crowley

MAP 6

114

CHAPTER VI

Lull and Flare-up

25 June–12 November 1951

After Mr. Malik made his proposal, the Peiping radio followed his lead and indicated that the rulers of Communist China favored a truce. President Truman then authorized General Ridgway to conduct negotiations with the enemy generals. The U.N. commander at once sent radio messages to his opposite numbers in the enemy camp, and after some argument both sides agreed to meet in Kaesong, a town near Korea's west coast about three miles south of the 38th parallel and between the opposing armies' front lines. After liaison officers had made preliminary arrangements, the negotiations opened on 10 July with Vice Adm. C. Turner Joy, the Far East naval commander, acting as chief delegate for the United Nations. Lt. Gen. Nam Il led the enemy delegation.

Both sides agreed that hostilities would continue until a truce was signed, but neither side was willing to start any large-scale offensives while the peace talks were in progress. All along the front—which now extended from the Imjin River to Ch'orwon, paralleled the base of the Iron Triangle, swung southeast to the lower edge of the Punchbowl, and then ran north and east to the Sea of Japan above Kansong—the fighting died down. U.N. troops busied themselves improving their positions and consolidating the ground they had just won.

Action was characterized by artillery fire and air strikes, plus a continuing bombardment of Wonsan. Combat patrols went out regularly; enemy attacks were repulsed. Offensive action consisted chiefly of limited regimental or battalion attacks designed to seize more favorable terrain, capture prisoners, and keep the enemy from nosing too close to the U.N. lines. With the exception of the flare-up in the fall of 1951 that followed the breaking-off of the truce negotiations in August, this general pattern was to prevail until just before the signing of the truce in 1953.

Enemy policy appeared to follow the same lines as that of the United Nations, whose intelligence officers concluded that the Chinese forces were being strengthened. New Chinese units were identified northeast of the Iron Triangle, in front of the IX Corps below Kumsong, and in the vicinity of the Punchbowl. The enemy, like the U.N. forces, appeared to be holding a main line of resistance with screening units in front rather than relying on defense by maneuver.

Throughout the summer months there was continuous, though local, fighting for limited objectives, and no day passed without casualties. In general the front lines remained stable except in the Iron Triangle and the Punchbowl. The Triangle action focused on the low Sobang Hills which the Chinese had reoccupied after being driven out during Van Fleet's June offensive. On 1 July tank-infantry task forces from the I Corps tried to eject the Chinese but failed. Repeating the attacks through Independence Day, tanks and infantry finally pushed the enemy entirely from the area between the Triangle's base and P'yonggang, then withdrew to the main U.N. line. At the same time I Corps patrols crossed the Imjin to harry the enemy, and the X Corps bombed and shelled positions in the Punchbowl where North Koreans appeared to be concentrating artillery and mortars.

Later in July Van Fleet ordered a northward advance in the X Corps zone to shorten the line, prevent the enemy from freely observing the KANSAS line, and force the enemy to pull back his mortars and artillery. The specific objective was a 3,890-foot-high mountain, designated Hill 1179 or Taeu-san, at the southwest edge of the Punchbowl which ROK marines had unsuccessfully attacked. It was defended by what was estimated to be a regiment (1,700 men) of North Koreans. Elements of the 2d Division, strongly supported by aircraft and artillery, took over and after a four-day assault secured the crest of Taeu-san.

In August the strength of all forces under Van Fleet's command numbered 586,769 at their peak. This figure included, in addition to 229,339 in the Eighth Army proper, 357,430 from the Republic of Korea, the U.S. Marines, the Fifth Air Force, and the seventeen other U.N. contingents. By now the Colombian Battalion had reached Korea to join in alongside the men from the United States, the Republic of Korea, Australia, Belgium, Canada, Ethiopia, France, Great Britain, Greece, India, the Netherlands, New Zealand, Norway, the Philippines, Sweden, Thailand, Turkey, and the Union of South Africa.

Action was focused again in the zone of the X Corps and the ROK I Corps to the east. Both corps, the latter supported by gunfire from warships lying offshore, advanced their fronts to gain more favorable terrain to the northeast and west of the Punchbowl, and the U.N. units on the western portion of the line sent out raiding parties and combat patrols to divert the enemy reserves. The X Corps and ROK I Corps offensives were carried out almost exclusively by South Koreans under American command and supported by American units. But on the night of 27–28 August, when a unit of the ROK 5th Division crumpled under an enemy counterattack delivered against a newly captured hill mass ("Bloody Ridge") west of the Punchbowl, the U.S. 9th Infantry Regiment of the 2d Division was committed. It was unable to retake the lost ground.

Late in August, after the truce negotiations had been suspended, Van Fleet determined to resume the offensive in order to drive the enemy farther back from the Hwach'on Reservoir (Seoul's source of water and electric power) and away from the Ch'orwon–Seoul railroad. Success in each of these enterprises would also straighten and shorten the U.N. front, give greater security to the KANSAS line, and inflict damage on the enemy. Therefore, when the 9th Infantry's attack failed, the U.N. commanders determined to put forth a major effort in the X Corps zone, using all five divisions in that corps to continue the ridge-top and mountain actions in the Punchbowl area.

The U.S. 1st Marine Division, with ROK marine units attached, opened a drive against the northern portion of the Punchbowl on 31 August. Two days later the 2d Division attacked northward against Bloody and Heartbreak Ridges in the vicinity of the Punchbowl's western edge and

Taeu-san. Both assaults, delivered uphill by burdened, straining infantrymen, met with initial success. By 3 September, the two divisions had reached their first objectives. Van Fleet ordered them to continue the advance as far north as the northwesterly leg of the Soyang River above the Punchbowl.

On 11 September the 1st Marine Division attacked again. After seven days of heavy fighting, with the enemy resolutely defending each ridge top from mutually supporting positions and yielding only after repeated counterattacks and seesaw struggles, the marines secured their objective on 18 September.[1]

Meanwhile the 2d Division, on Bloody and Heartbreak Ridges west of the Punchbowl, was engaged in the fiercest action since spring. Like the marines, the 2d Division infantrymen, often carrying 60-mm. mortar or 75-mm. recoilless rifle rounds as well as their own ammunition and equipment, crawled hand over hand up towering, knife-crested ridges to assault the hard-fighting enemy who would yield a ridge only in desperation, then strike back in vigorous counterattack. The same crest often changed hands several times each day.

By 19 September the X Corps front was stabilized except in the 2d Division's zone. Supplied by airdrop and by sturdy Korean carriers with A-frames strapped to their backs, and heavily supported by aircraft and artillery, the 2d Division fought on bitterly. In one instance it delivered, within the space of twenty-four hours, no less than eleven separate assaults, all unsuccessful, against one ridge. The battle raged into October. Finally, on the 14th, after the enemy seemed to be willing to reopen the truce talks, the last ridge was secured and the 2d Division consolidated its hard-won gains.

Along the western portion of the front, action in September was characterized by local attacks, counterattacks, and combat patrols which culminated, in the eastern portion of the Triangle, in a series of successful raids by tank-infantry task forces from the IX Corps. Once these were accomplished, the five divisions—the ROK 1st, the 1st British Commonwealth, the U.S. 1st Cavalry, 3d, and 25th Divisions—struck north across a forty-mile front from the Kaesong area to Ch'orwon to advance the front three or four miles, establish a new line, JAMESTOWN, and thus protect the Ch'orwon–Seoul railroad. By 12 October JAMESTOWN was secured. The IX Corps, to the right, followed with aggressive patrolling toward Kumsong. By 21 October the 24th Division had seized the commanding heights just south of Kumsong. The successful advances of August, September, and October gave the U.N. forces possession of commanding ground along their entire front, and may have influenced the enemy leaders to decide to sit down at the peace table once again.

General Ridgway had attempted to persuade the enemy to resume negotiating on 4 October, while the 2d Division was fighting hard west of the Punchbowl. Six days later liaison officers met again, this time at Panmunjom, a tiny village on the Seoul highway north of the Imjin River. Their deliberations were interrupted by a misdirected U.N. air attack near Panmunjom that brought from the enemy a violent protest. It was 22 October before the liaison officers met again, and three days later the plenipotentiaries once more resumed the negotiations that were to continue for many weary months. Meanwhile, for the soldier at the front, the war went on.

---

[1] Several days later the marines tried the first troop lift by helicopter in a combat zone. During September they moved company-sized units, and in October managed to move a whole battalion.

SECTION 4

22 April–19 May 1951

U.N. Forces Withdrawing Under the Weight of the Enemy Offensive. Top, Belgian Battalion heading south; middle, British 29th Brigade resting along the roadside; bottom, 24th Infantry Division moving to new defensive positions.

Top, 65th Infantry, 3d Division, moving down a
valley road; middle, M46 Patton tank towing a
crippled mate through Uijongbu; bottom, battalion commander calling in the position of his men
near Uijongbu.

F-80 SHOOTING STAR BOMBING ENEMY POSI-
TIONS south of Ch'orwon.

"LONG TOMS" OF THE 204TH FIELD ARTIL-
LERY BATTALION firing north of Seoul.

25TH DIVISION MEN IN THE HILLS south of Ch'orwon expecting an enemy attack, 23 April.

Infantryman of 24th Regiment Squeezing One Off, west central sector.

Cleaning Out Enemy Emplacements. Note Hant'an River in background.

Escorting a Wounded 25th Division Infantryman down the hill to an aid station, 22 April.

F-9F Pantherjets Returning to the Carrier USS *PRINCETON* (left center) after a bombing mission. USS *Philippine Sea* is in the right background.

AD Skyraider on the deck of the USS *Princeton* lowering its wings as it swings into take-off position.

The Hwach'on Dam Under Attack by Navy AD Skyraiders using aerial torpedoes.

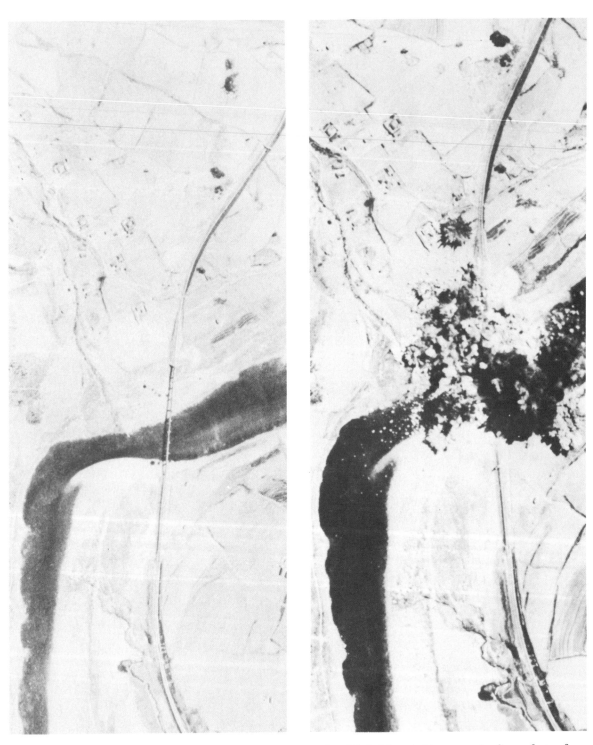

RAILROAD BRIDGE ACROSS THE TAEDONG RIVER, south of Tokch'on, is blown up by Superforts of the Far East Air Forces, May 1951.

128

MARSHALING YARD NEAR YANGYANG on east coast undergoing a bombing attack by B-26 light bombers of the Fifth Air Force.

SECTION 5

20 May–24 June 1951

17TH INFANTRY, 7TH DIVISION, TAKING TIME OUT along a road near Chungbangdae-ni, south of the Hongch'on River, 22 May.

MARINE PATROL CLOSING IN ON A KOREAN HUT. Note feet of enemy casualty in the doorway. U.N. offensive, opened on 18 May, was slowed by heavy rains, mud, and stiff enemy resistance.

HIGH-LEVEL CONFERENCE. From left, Maj. Gen. William M. Hoge, Commanding General, IX Corps; Maj. Gen. Blackshear M. Bryan, Commanding General, 24th Division; Lt. Gen. James A. Van Fleet, Commanding General, U.S. Eighth Army; and General Ridgway.

31st Infantry Regiment, 7th Division, on a hill near Ch'unch'on, 24 May. Note 57-mm. recoilless rifles in photograph above. A casualty (opposite page, bottom) receives emergency first aid. On the 25th, elements of the 7th Division moved north of Ch'unch'on.

SUPPLIES FOR THE 187TH REGIMENTAL COMBAT TEAM dropping near Umyang-ni, south of Inje.

AIRDROPPED SUPPLIES NEAR THE MAIN SUPPLY ROUTE south of Inje. On 27 May, the 187th drove into Inje.

MOVING OUT UNDER ENEMY FIRE, 26 May.

ROK 8TH DIVISION MEN ON THEIR WAY FORWARD passing combat-worn troops resting on their way to the rear.

ROK 16TH REGIMENT ADVANCING to positions held by 7th Infantry.

EVACUATING 2D DIVISION CASUALTIES across the Soyang River.

M4 Tanks of 1st Cavalry Division fording the Imjin River.

Enemy-Made Footbridge used by 7th Infantry, 3d Division, in withdrawing from the front lines.

CHINESE PRISONERS captured north of the Imjin River by 1st Cavalry Division.

PUERTO RICAN INFANTRYMEN, 65th Infantry, 3d Division, in an enemy-made trench, 1 June.

COMPANY I, 5TH CAVALRY REGIMENT, moving across rice fields before starting the climb up Hill 513, north of Tokchong, 1 June.

OBSERVATION PLANE SEARCHING THE RUGGED PEAKS for information on enemy positions to relay to ground troops.

F-80 SHOOTING STAR on a strafing mission north of Inje, 1 June.

Medium Tank M4A3 Firing at enemy positions in the hills north of Inje, 4 June.

Engineers Probing for Enemy Mines ahead of a creeping tank south of Ch'orwon, 10 June.

MINE EXPLOSION CASUALTY AWAITING EVACUATION BY HELICOPTER. Above, medical corpsmen administer plasma to one of five marines wounded in the explosion. Right page: top, a Sikorsky helicopter approaches a marker placed as a landing guide; bottom, marines hold down the helicopter after it lands on the windy slope.

HAULING IN A "PIG" aboard the mine sweeper USS *Mocking Bird*. This device, properly termed a paravane, is used in minesweeping operations.

U.S. NAVY HOSPITAL SHIP *Haven* docked at Pusan. Denmark, India, Italy, Norway, and Sweden also furnished special medical elements for the U.N. effort in Korea.

USS *NEW JERSEY* Firing Off the East Coast of Korea. Below is a close-up of the 16-inch guns aboard the ship. Enemy-held east coast is barely visible in background.

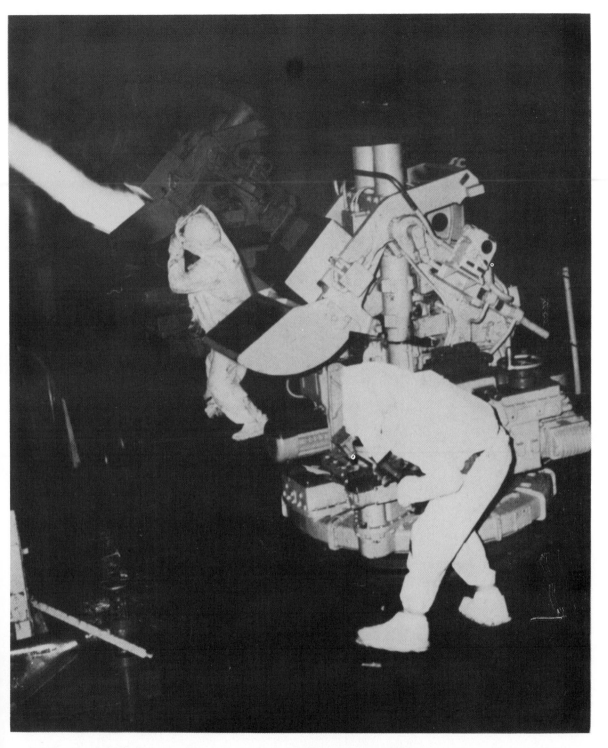

"MEN FROM MARS" FIRING ROCKETS AT ENEMY-HELD WONSAN. The men are wearing one-piece suits, with hood and gloves, made of plastic-coated glass fabric designed to give head-to-toe protection against back blasts of fuming acids.

MARINES PUSHING FORWARD. By 9 June the 1st Marine Division had advanced north of Yanggu, east central front.

RECOILLESS RIFLE CREW, 7th Cavalry Regiment, firing near Ch'orwon.

Trying To Ward Off the Deafening Blast of a 75-mm. Recoilless Rifle

"I don't care how accurate it is, get rid of it!"

DIRECT HIT ON AN ENEMY WAREHOUSE IN WONSAN

B-26 Invader Over a Target in North Korea

Napalm Bomb Attack on an Enemy Industrial Center

SECTION 6

25 June–12 November 1951

Riflemen of the 7th Infantry, 3d Division, Moving Out To Attack Hill 717, south of P'yonggang in the Iron Triangle, 3 July.

UNITED NATIONS DELEGATION AT KAESONG. From left: Maj. Gen. Laurence C. Craigie, USAF; Maj. Gen. Paik Sun Yup, Commanding General, ROK I Corps; Vice Adm. C. Turner Joy, Far East Naval Commander (acting as chief delegate for the U.N.); Maj. Gen. Henry I. Hodes, Deputy Chief of Staff, U.S. Eighth Army; and Rear Adm. Arleigh A. Burke, U.S.N.

CONFERENCE SITE IN KAESONG. Photograph was taken 10 July 1951, the day negotiations opened.

ENEMY DELEGATION AT CONFERENCE SITE. From left: Maj. Gen. Hsieh Fang and Lt. Gen. Teng Hua, Chinese Army; Lt. Gen. Nam Il, chief delegate for the Communists; Maj. Gen. Lee Sang Cho and Maj. Gen. Chang Pyong San, North Korean Army.

SIGNAL CORPS MEN REPAIRING COMMUNICATIONS LINES in a mountain pass south of Hwach'on.

F-86 Sabrejets Ready To Take Off for "Mig Alley," an area in North Korea where Russian-built MIG-15 jets were frequently encountered.

Arriving at X Corps Headquarters for a Liaison Visit, July 1951. Lt. Gen. Harold R. Bull (left), Commandant of the National War College, and Maj. Gen. Orlando Ward (center), Chief of Military History, talk with Maj. Gen. Clovis E. Byers, Commanding General, U.S. X Corps.

GENERAL BYERS VISITING A COMMAND POST in the 2d Division area.

ENGINEERS REPAIRING ROAD DAMAGE caused by heavy rain near Inje, 21 July.

Trucks Heading for Inje along newly repaired road, 1 August.

STRETCHER-BEARERS ACCOMPANYING TROOPS UP HILL 1179, southwest edge of the Punchbowl.

WALKING WOUNDED FROM 38TH INFANTRY going down Hill 1179 to an aid station. On 30 July elements of the 2d Division seized Taeu-san (Hill 1179).

ENEMY SOLDIERS CAPTURED IN THE PUNCHBOWL AREA are searched at command post of the 2d Battalion, 16th Infantry, ROK 8th Division.

ORPHANED KOREAN CHILDREN received money, clothing, food, and toys contributed by thousands of Americans.

KOREAN LABORER CARRYING EMPTY SHELL CONTAINERS on an A-frame. Because of poor roads and hilly terrain, the A-frame, an ancient native wooden pack carrier, became indispensable for supplying many forward units.

LST LOADED WITH BOXCARS moving into Pusan harbor, August 1951.

170

CRANE UNLOADING A BOXCAR AT PUSAN

F-84 THUNDERJETS, securely anchored aboard a carrier, en route to Japan for action over Korea.

GIANT CRANE loading a mobile crane onto a barge for shipment to Korea.

MEN OF THE 23D INFANTRY trying to save equipment in the swollen Soyang River.

PONTON BRIDGE IN 3D DIVISION SECTOR washed several hundred yards downstream by flash floods. During August heavy torrential rains bogged down lines of communication to the front.

AID STATION housed in bunkers along the side of a mountain.

OBSERVATION POST, 36TH REGIMENT, ROK 10TH DIVISION, 20 August. One week later the 36th Regiment abandoned its positions, returning to Worun-ni, south of Hill 1179.

175

KOREAN LABORERS helping to carry 75-mm. recoilless rifles up to 2d Division troops.

WEARY SOLDIERS OF THE 9TH INFANTRY REGIMENT moving to new positions near Yanggu. In late August the 9th Infantry fought at Bloody Ridge, west of the Punchbowl.

"Hello service battery? You better get hold of some ord-
nance people and come on up here. Somebody's fouled up
somewhere!"

GUN CREW OF BATTERY C, 204TH FIELD ARTILLERY BATTALION, firing a 155-mm. self-propelled
gun at enemy positions north of Yonch'on.

CLOUDS OF SMOKE FROM PRECISION BOMBING of enemy marshaling yards after a surprise attack by thirty-five B-29 Superforts, 25 August. The yards are at Rashin, seventeen miles south of the USSR boundary on the northeast coast of Korea.

HELICOPTER LANDING ON FLIGHT DECK of the USS *Boxer* after an air-sea rescue mission.

REFUELING IN SEA OF JAPAN. A Navy tanker (center) is servicing a destroyer (left) and a cruiser (right).

Up the Steep Slope of Hill 940 trudges Company F, 9th Infantry.

RIFLE TEAM FIRING AT AN ENEMY POSITION with a 57-mm. recoilless rifle.

QUAD .50's giving support to the 9th Infantry fighting for Bloody Ridge.

NEAR THE CREST OF BLOODY RIDGE. This position changed hands several times during September.

Hill 983, crest of Bloody Ridge.

Firing an 81-mm. Mortar at enemy positions on Hill 931, 13 September.

"You seen our pack mule?"

TROOPS USING PACK ANIMALS to carry supplies.

Fire Direction and Control Team of the 23d Infantry within view of Hill 931, crest of Heartbreak Ridge, in background.

TAEU-SAN
(1179)

PUNCHBOWL

HEARTBREAK RIDGE

Company E, 23d Infantry, on Its Way to Hill 931 to relieve Company C, which had been fighting on the ridge for nine days. One of the men rests near an enemy casualty, below.

French Battalion Troops Attached to 2d Division occupying Hill 931, 23 September.

CASUALTIES OF FIGHT FOR HILL 931 receiving medical attention at an aid station in 2d Division area.

M4 Tanks firing in support of the 2d Division, north of Pia-ri near Hill 1179, 18 September.

105-mm. Howitzer Mounted on Gun Motor Carriage M7 firing in support of the 1st Marine Division, 22 September.

PLOWING THROUGH MUD NEAR KUMSONG, 21 September. Leading vehicle is a multiple-gun motor carriage M16, better known as Quad .50's.

GUN CREW LOADING A CAMOUFLAGED 105-MM. HOWITZER used in support of the 7th Marine Regiment.

ENEMY CASUALTY NEAR BUNKER overrun by 7th Marine Regiment. Note trees sheared off by artillery fire.

SIKORSKY HELICOPTER HOVERING OVER HILL 884 with supplies, 20 September. During September the marines moved company-sized units by helicopter; in October they moved units the size of a battalion.

POSITIONS ON THE MAIN LINE OF RESISTANCE occupied by the Colombian Battalion, attached to the 24th Division, near Chup'a-ri overlooking the Kumsong Valley.

194

SUPPLIES AND REINFORCEMENTS FOR THE ROK 21ST REGIMENT in a cove near the Hwach'on Reservoir.

BRIDGE OVER UNDERCUT ON ROAD BETWEEN INJE AND YANGGU. Engineers removed bridge after filling the undercut area to road level.

GENERAL OF THE ARMY OMAR N. BRADLEY, Chairman of the Joint Chiefs of Staff, at 7th Division headquarters area. From the left: Lt. Gen. William M. Hoge, Commanding General, IX Corps; General Bradley; Maj. Gen. Ira P. Swift, Commanding General, 25th Infantry Division; Maj. Gen. Frank F. Everest, Commanding General, 5th Air Force (shaking hands with General Bradley).

MAJ. GEN. CLOVIS E. BYERS (left, foreground), Commanding General, U.S. X Corps, with Brig. Gen. Min Ki Sik, Commanding General, ROK 5th Division, on the way to a training demonstration.

GENERAL RIDGWAY, Commander in Chief, United Nations Command (left), with Maj. Gen. Claude B. Ferenbaugh, Commanding General, 7th Infantry Division, 2 October 1951.

Loading a DUKW From a Victory Ship, Inch'on harbor, 3 November. The DUKW will transfer its cargo directly to railroad cars.

Korean Workers Loading Gondolas with artillery ammunition for the front.

Cargo Net Filled With Turkeys for Thanksgiving Day dinner.

USS *NEW JERSEY* along the North Korean coast firing all nine of her 16-inch guns, November 1951.

12 NOVEMBER 1951–30 JUNE 1952

CHAPTER VII

Stalemate

12 November 1951–30 June 1952

As the year 1951 drew to a close the character of the conflict returned to that of July and early August. Fighting tapered off into a monotonous routine of patrol clashes, raids, and bitter small-unit struggles for key outpost positions. By the end of the year a lull had settled over the battlefield with the opposing sides deployed along defense lines that spanned the breadth of the peninsula. Not until the early summer of 1953 was the fighting resumed on a larger scale, and then only briefly.

The lull resulted from General Ridgway's decision to halt offensive ground operations in Korea. Two factors influenced his decision: the cost of further major assaults on the enemy's defenses would be more than the results would justify; and the possibility that peace might come out of the recently reopened armistice talks ruled out the mounting of any costly large-scale offensive by either side. His orders to Van Fleet, therefore, issued on 12 November 1951, were to cease offensive operations and begin an active defense of the Eighth Army's front. Attacks were to be limited to those necessary for strengthening the main line of resistance and for establishing an outpost line 3,000–5,000 yards forward of the main positions.

The line to be defended was manned by three American and one South Korean corps and extended from the Yellow Sea in a great arc eastward for 155 miles to the shores of the Sea of Japan. Defending the army's left wing, the U.S. I Corps, now commanded by Lt. Gen. John W. O'Daniel, occupied the sector originating at the confluence of the Imjin and Han Rivers and extending northeast to a point midway between Ch'orwon and Kumhwa. On the U.S. I Corps right flank the defenses of Maj. Gen. Willard G. Wyman's U.S. IX Corps began, bulging northward toward Kumsong and east to the Pukhan River, which formed the corps' right boundary. East of the Pukhan the U.S. X Corps, under Maj. Gen. Clovis E. Byers from 15 July to 5 December and thereafter under Maj. Gen. Williston B. Palmer, extended its lines eastward over the mountainous spine of the peninsula to the Nam River, to meet the left boundary of the ROK I Corps. This latter corps, commanded by the ROK Army's Maj. Gen. Paik Sun Yup, defended the Eighth Army's right wing; its zone extended due north along the Korean east coast from the Nam River to Kosong.

Action on the Eighth Army front during the last two months of the year was limited mostly to patrol clashes and repelling light enemy attacks. Blanketed by U.N. harassing artillery fire, the enemy moved only at night, and his own artillery was restricted by the liberal use of U.N. counterbattery fire. In the U.S. I Corps sector the ROK 1st Division mounted a series of tank-infantry raids against enemy positions in the area south of Panmunjom, but after 16 December these small-scale actions gave way once more to patrolling.

The third week of December saw a series of changes on both sides. The U.S. 45th Division, the first National Guard division to fight in Korea, arrived from Japan and replaced the 1st Cavalry Division north of Seoul in the I Corps sector. The 1st Cavalry Division returned to Japan for a well-earned rest. Following up this change the U.S. 2d Division, which had been in IX Corps reserve, relieved the U.S. 25th Division on the line.

On the enemy side, Eighth Army intelligence reported, the North Korean *I Corps* had moved from its positions on the western sector of the enemy battle front to reserve positions in the eastern sector. As a result the Chinese now defended the entire western and central parts of the enemy line. This concentration of the North Korean forces in the rugged eastern sector, where there was little likelihood of a major U.N. thrust, indicated that the North Korean Army might be suffering from a manpower shortage.

The air conflict over Korea continued at a slower pace as snow, fog, and heavy cloud cover reduced visibility, but sorties averaged 700 daily. Enemy pilots seemed reluctant to close with American Sabres. Either their losses had begun to tell, or a new group was being pushed through a jet training cycle and the enemy flyers were not ready to do battle with the Sabres. U.N. bombers and fighter-bombers continued their interdiction campaign, Operation STRANGLE,

against railroad tracks, bridges, and highway traffic.

At sea, naval units of nine nations tightened their blockade around the coast line of North Korea. Naval planes from the fast U.S. carriers *Antietam* and *Valley Forge* bombed the rail systems around Yonghung, blasted bridges, and blew up boxcars. A landing ship, equipped with 5-inch rockets, joined in the bombardment of the northeast port city of Songjin. Two thousand rockets fell on the harbor area to destroy a large supply point, shunting yards, and bridges while coastal roadways were raked with shell fragments. United States destroyers continued to bombard Wonsan while the cruiser *Saint Paul*, supporting the ROK I Corps at the eastern extremity of the front, fired on targets of opportunity. Off the west coast, south and west of Chinnamp'o, the British light cruiser *Belfast*, the U.S. destroyer *Eversole*, and the British frigates *Mounts Bay* and *White Sand Bay* scored direct hits on three enemy gun emplacements and blew up a small arms supply depot.

On the ground, patrols from both sides were out in force. As expected, the enemy jumped off in a series of small-scale attacks during Christmas week. The initial thrust, delivered by about a battalion, came in the X Corps sector deep in the eastern mountains. Covered by 82-mm. mortar and artillery fire, the enemy captured an outpost of the ROK 3d Division. Two counterattacks failed, but on 28 December a battalion of the ROK 3d restored the outpost position and enemy attacks stopped. That afternoon action erupted on the far left flank of the otherwise quiet front. A Chinese battalion, its members wearing white parkas in the snow-covered terrain, lashed out at a company-held outpost of the ROK 1st Division that served as a patrol base for the division. A forty-minute pitched battle ensued in bitter, subzero weather before the ROK company fell back. Two days later, tank-supported elements of the ROK 1st won back 900 yards of the ground the company had lost but failed to recapture the outpost itself. The high ground was secured by the last day of the year in spite of bad weather and heavy enemy resistance that cut short the attack.

Although the decision by General Ridgway to discontinue offensive operations changed the Eighth Army's mission to one of defense, he had not implied that all action should cease. His order did not preclude raids, attritional warfare, or local limited offensives under favorable conditions. Therefore in December 1951, Van Fleet directed his corps commanders to make their attacks against enemy positions as costly to the foe as possible. Later, at a meeting with the corps commanders, he directed them to begin attacking with artillery and air strikes to impress the Chinese and North Koreans with the tremendous fire power of the Eighth Army. As the new year began, the Eighth Army made ready to carry out these instructions.

The 155-mile front remained generally quiet in the opening days of 1952, although patrols were regularly dispatched to gain prisoners and information. The most significant activity during the first month of the year occurred in the western extremity of the I Corps line. When light counterblows had failed to dislodge the Chinese from a ROK 1st Division outpost, the division opened a co-ordinated attack on the height on 3 January. After a five-day struggle, the infantry succeeded in seizing and securing the hill and adjacent positions. The Chinese lost heavily in this action, suffering an estimated 4,000 casualties and the destruction of a considerable amount of precious equipment and supplies.

In January 1952 the Eighth Army opened a month-long artillery-air campaign against enemy positions. The artillery units of the four corps fired on remunerative targets, and on alternate days U.N. aircraft struck at others with high explosives and fire bombs. Thousands of rounds of artillery shells and bombs fell on the targets during the month. No doubt this artillery-air attack discouraged enemy offensive action, but the strength of the enemy's positions and his skill in camouflage minimized its effect.

The superiority of U.N. air and artillery fire forced the Chinese and North Koreans to dig in deeply. Simple emplacements became dirt and log fortifications with overhead cover that varied from four to fifteen feet in thickness. It was common practice to place primary defense positions on the forward slope of a hill and dig personnel shelters, artillery emplacements, command posts, and supply points, all well-camouflaged, on the reverse slope. Tunnels or covered trenches connected the fighting positions with the shelters. Thus enemy troops could move to the shelters when attacked by aircraft or artillery, then return to their positions when the fire lifted. All positions afforded cover from high-angle fire and provided good fields of fire.

U.N. artillery and the infantry's recoilless weapons, employing direct fire, neutralized many of the positions on the forward slopes of hills but were less effective against enemy fortifications on the reverse slopes. Many times the shells would fall into the valley below rather than on the target. The aerial fire bomb was no more effective. Only a direct hit from a 500- or 1,000-pound bomb would destroy these emplacements.

Sporadic, light ground action continued to mark the fighting during the remainder of January and February of 1952. Patrols went out daily to feel out the enemy, capture prisoners, and locate enemy positions. The newly arrived 45th Division carried out a number of tank-infantry raids near the end of January to destroy enemy positions and seize prisoners. Various ruses aimed at luring the enemy out of his positions met with little or no success.

While the spring rains and mists that cloaked Korea in March and April limited air and ground operations, Van Fleet shifted his units along the front to give the South Korean Army a greater share of responsibility for defending the battle line and to concentrate American fire power in the vulnerable western sector.

By 1 May the 1st Marine Division had moved from the Punchbowl area in the U.S. X Corps zone to replace the ROK 1st Division in General O'Daniel's I Corps. Here the marines' amphibious training and equipment could be utilized to conduct small raids across the Imjin River. The ROK 1st Division, after nine weeks training, replaced the U.S. 3d Division in the corps' right center sector. General O'Daniel now had the 1st Marine Division on the left wing, the 1st British Commonwealth and the ROK 1st in the center, and the 45th on the right.

General Van Fleet made more extensive changes on the central front. He erased the U.S. I Corps–U.S. IX Corps boundary and redrew it farther west. At the same time he also had the right boundary of the latter corps moved west. With this shift General Wyman's IX Corps, by 1 May, consisted of the ROK 9th Division on the left, the U.S. 7th Division in the center, and the U.S. 40th Division on the right. The 40th, the second National Guard division to fight in Korea, arrived in late January 1952. Assigned to the IX Corps, it relieved the U.S.

24th Division, which returned to Japan. On the IX Corps' right flank, into the gap created by the shift in boundary, Van Fleet moved the reactivated ROK II Corps. The new corps' battle front, defended on the left by the ROK 6th Division, in the center by the ROK Capital, and on the right by the ROK 3rd, extended eastward from Kumsong to the X Corps boundary.

Only two changes occurred on the east central and eastern fronts. In General Palmer's X Corps, the ROK 8th replaced the 1st Marine Division. General Palmer's sector now had the ROK 7th Division on the left wing, the U.S. 25th in the center, and the ROK 8th on the right wing. On the eastern front, the ROK 11th Division moved up from its training area and took over defense of the left half of the ROK I Corps zone, while the ROK 5th assumed responsibility for the right sector on the Sea of Japan.

Ground action had continued to be limited to patrols in March and April, but the enemy became bolder in May. He increased his probing attacks and patrols, intensified his artillery fire, and aggressively intercepted U.N. patrols. The increased enemy activity was most pronounced in the U.S. I Corps sector, where the Chinese executed thirty probing attacks, all unsuccessful, during May against the ROK 1st Division. But Chinese thrusts in the 45th Division sector overshadowed all other action across the entire front. When the Chinese made three raids against the 45th, the U.S. division countered by sending nine tanks of the 245th Tank Battalion and a ROK infantry unit to raid the town of Agok, eight miles west of Ch'orwon, on 25 May. That night the Chinese launched an unsuccessful attack against one of the division's patrol bases. Three nights later two Chinese companies intercepted a patrol from the 279th

Infantry Regiment, on the division's right. Cut off, the patrol engaged the enemy with small arms and automatic weapons fire and radioed for assistance. Although the Chinese fired nearly three hundred mortar and artillery rounds on the main line of resistance, a relief platoon started out immediately and reached the besieged patrol three hours later. When aircraft illuminated the battle area with flares, the enemy's fire lessened. Finding the patrol reinforced and the battlefield light as day, the Chinese broke off the engagement and withdrew.

The enemy's increased aggressiveness was greatly aided by his growing strength in artillery. In July 1951 the enemy had fired an estimated 8,000 artillery and mortar rounds, but in May 1952 an estimated total of 102,000 rounds fell on the Eighth Army's positions. Furthermore, the firing was more effective. The Chinese and North Koreans showed ability to mass eight to ten guns on a target, and to place counter-battery fire accurately. They fired widely spaced alternating guns and moved their artillery pieces frequently. In May the Chinese also moved artillery forward to within 2,000–6,000 yards of the Eighth Army's defenses.

As a result of increased Chinese ground activity at the hinge of the Eighth Army's line west of Ch'orwon, Maj. Gen. David L. Ruffner, the 45th Division commander, planned an operation to establish eleven patrol bases across his division's front. If his plan succeeded these bases would screen the division's main line of resistance more adequately by denying the enemy their use. This operation, known as Operation COUNTER, began on 6 June when the two front-line regiments of the division launched a series of attacks to occupy the eleven objectives. By 7 June all but one objective had

fallen to the assault units of the division. The enemy followed up with a series of counterblows during the next five days, but these were successfully repulsed.

Seven days later, 13 June, the 45th Division opened Phase II of COUNTER to seize the last objective, a hill which the 45th had abandoned in March. It lay at the southern tip of a T-shaped ridge line eight miles west and slightly north of Ch'orwon. The struggle for the height began with an air strike and a preparatory artillery bombardment. The 2d Battalion of the 180th Infantry then crossed the line of departure and engaged the Chinese at close quarters. American infantry repulsed four company-size Chinese counterattacks. Next day the regiment's 3d Battalion relieved the 2d and secured the objective. U.N. aircraft flew fifty-eight close-support missions during the first eighteen hours, and U.N. guns fired 43,600 rounds during the forty-eight-hour battle. At noon on 14 June, Phase II of Plan COUNTER ended with the new chain of patrol bases one half to two miles in front of the main line of resistance secure in the division's hands.

The Chinese immediately launched counterattacks along the entire front of the 45th Division. They first expended about two battalions in futile efforts to retake Hill 191. Then, on the night of 20–21 June, they opened a regimental assault, supported by 5,000 rounds of artillery and mortar fire, against Hill 255, southwest of Hill 191. When this failed they struck at outpost positions on the western anchor of the division's outpost line, climaxing their efforts on the night of 28–29 June with an unsuccessful attack that lasted four and a half hours. Throughout June the 45th sustained 1,004 casualties, but the Chinese lost an estimated 5,000 men, including thirty captured.

Patrol clashes and light probing attacks

by the enemy marked the action elsewhere on the front during May and June. Strong positions and the mountainous terrain acted as deterrents to any large-scale action on the central and eastern fronts.

If ground action waned during the first half of 1952, so did air action. Enemy jet pilots had flown 3,700 sorties in January 1952 but only 308 in June. Even though the Chinese and North Koreans put fewer and fewer operational aircraft into the air, they continued to expand their air potential. U.N. intelligence estimated that they had a total of 1,000 planes, including 400 jets, in Manchuria and China during May 1951, but twelve months later they were reported as possessing 1,800 planes, including 1,000 jets, in the same areas. The enemy also tightened his night air defenses. Over a dozen of his cannon- and rocket-firing jets attacked ten B-29's on the night of 10–11 June as the U.N. aircraft were carrying out a bombing raid on the Kwaksan railroad bridge south of the Yalu River. Assisted by radar-controlled searchlights, the jets shot down one bomber and caused a second to make a forced landing.

Throughout the first half of 1952, then, the U.N. forces waged a war of containment. U.N. infantry units parried enemy thrusts and launched attacks of their own, while naval units blockaded the coasts of North Korea and established an anti-invasion patrol to protect ROK partisans holding offshore islands. Sabrejets successfully limited hostile aircraft to the area north of the Ch'ongch'on River line, and friendly bombers interdicted hostile supply lines. The front-line soldier continued to watch for enemy assaults while hoping that the armistice negotiators would soon reach agreement.

CHAPTER VIII

Support and Service

The prosecution of the war in Korea called for a tremendous administrative and logistical effort on the part of the Eighth Army. Decisions in Washington and Tokyo required that the army not only carry on its tactical mission but operate the supply lines within the peninsula, administer the rear areas, give relief to the disrupted civilian population, and run the prisoner of war camps until August 1952—tasks normally carried out by the theater headquarters.[1] In addition, the Eighth Army had to integrate the multinational forces fighting in Korea within its command structure. Multitudinous problems arose in carrying out these various responsibilities.

To integrate the ground contingents offered by member countries of the United Nations most efficiently, the U.N. commander's plan was to assign them, according to their size, to American units within the Eighth Army. Thus the Turkish Brigade came under control of an American division. The United Kingdom's two brigades and the one from Canada were placed under army control until July 1951, when the 1st British Commonwealth Division was formed and assumed control of all Commonwealth forces in Korea. This division, in turn, came under operational control of an American corps. Since all other ground combat units were of battalion size, they were attached to U.S. infantry regiments.

A number of problems required immediate solution. Language barriers, different standards of training, divergent tactical concepts, variations in dietary habits, dissimilar religious and national customs, and other discrepancies had to be reconciled. Some were resolved with little or no difficulty; others required extensive planning for solution.

The difficulties experienced when the first U.N. contingents came to Korea led the Eighth Army to organize the United Nations Reception Center. The center became responsible for clothing and equipping U.N. forces upon their arrival in Korea and for providing them with familiarization training in American arms and equipment. As the newcomers went through the reception center, American officers could evaluate their proficiency. These officers soon learned that some of the units were not so well trained as advance reports had indicated and that some lacked aggressiveness. As a result, the familiarization training programs were expanded.

Training and other factors influenced the assignment and subsequent role of the U.N. contingents, although the most desirable

---

[1] In August 1952, the Eighth Army was relieved of these tasks when the Far East Command organized the Korean Communications Zone, under its direct control, for this purpose.

course of action was to employ all U.N. units exactly as similar U.S. units were employed. Those units whose training did not approximate U.S. standards and who did not develop satisfactorily received additional training while on line of communications guard duty before being committed. Troops not naturally aggressive and under poor leadership were not given an assault role in the attack. Those lacking in soldierly steadfastness did not receive key defense missions. But most U.N. units were considered capable of executing any tactical mission appropriate for a similar U.S. unit.

In assigning the U.N. units and in giving them missions U.S. commanders had to reckon with divergent staff and tactical concepts and techniques. One unit preferred organizing the high ground when on the defense, whereas American doctrine favored organizing the forward slopes to obtain maximum effect with grazing and interlocking fire from automatic weapons. Another unit considered reconnaissance in force and combat patrols wasteful in that casualties were suffered without the compensatory gain of a physical objective. Some units did not think in terms of massed fire power to the degree U.S. forces did. There were other minor variations, but generally the non-U.S. units endeavored to pattern their actions after those of their American counterparts. Most of the U.N. officers from other countries, particularly staff officers, had attended various U.S. service schools. They were thus familiar with American tactical doctrine, and their military concepts and practices were generally in accord with it.

With so many nationalities operating under a unified command in Korea it was only natural that language difficulties should develop. Although the language problem was never completely solved, it did not interfere with the army's tactical operations. English was the official language, and all orders, directives, and instructions were issued in that tongue. The task of translation fell on the non-U.S. contingents for they had enough men that knew English well, whereas the American commands to which the contingents were attached had too few soldiers that were competent in a language other than their own. The integrated U.N. units also furnished liaison officers to these same American commands.

In theory it would have been desirable to have each U.N. country furnish the necessary logistical support for the men whom it sent into the conflict in Korea. In practice, however, it was simpler to have the United States furnish the support on a reimbursable basis. Thus the Eighth Army, which had the responsibility for supplying all of the units integrated into it, could do the job via a single line of communications instead of many. Nonetheless it encountered a number of difficulties.

National differences in customs and tastes led to many complications in supplying U.N. forces with rations. Because of Moslem religious restrictions, the Turks could not eat pork or pork products. The Hindus of the Indian contingent could not eat beef because of similar restrictions. The Turks wanted strong coffee, spices, and butter instead of margarine. The Hindus had to have rice, curry powder, and strong spices. Thailanders and Filipinos required rice, strong spices, and strong tea and coffee. The Dutch missed their milk and cheese, and the French their bottle of wine. Nearly all of the Europeans wanted a great deal more bread than the American ration provided. The Japan Logistical Command Quartermaster modified the ration to meet these various requirements.

Types of provisions furnished to particular countries changed from time to time, but in May 1952 only three countries—Canada, Norway, and Sweden—were accepting the complete American ration with nothing taken away or added. British Commonwealth forces, other than the Canadians, received all food supplies except perishables from British Commonwealth sources. All other units depended fully on the United States for their food supplies, with the rations modified to suit their tastes and customs.

Items of American clothing generally won the favor of the U.N. troops from other countries, though many of them were not convinced that two layers of light clothing were better for winter than a single layer of heavy clothing. The major problem was in measurements. Western Europeans are of about the same size as Americans; so are the Greeks and Turks, though their wider feet made fitting of shoes difficult. Oriental troops such as the Thailanders and Filipinos, on the other hand, are considerably smaller and their clothing had to be cut down. For them too, fitting of shoes was a problem, especially for the Thailanders.

Supplying the integrated units was part of the generally difficult task of the Eighth Army in carrying out its overall logistical mission. The logistical responsibility held by the army involved operating the ports and railways, receiving and classifying the incoming supplies and equipment, and forwarding them to the battle front. To organize and control this logistical effort, the Eighth Army formed the 2d Logistical Command. This command also took over the job of administering the rear areas.

Logistical support of an army in the field is an arduous task, even under ideal conditions. In South Korea, conditions were far from ideal. The country has only one port—Pusan—considered adequate to handle incoming military supplies. The mountainous east coast and the extreme tidal range of the west coast prohibit construction of adequate ports. Inch'on, the port for Seoul, and several smaller ports on the west and south coast were available, but deep-draft vessels had to remain offshore and have their cargoes lightered in. Hence Pusan became the major port for the Eighth Army and received nearly all supplies.

There were disadvantages in using Pusan as the chief port. It is located at the extreme southeast tip of the peninsula. As the Eighth Army moved northward its supply line was correspondingly extended. The lack of adequate railroads and highways from Pusan to the battle front added to the burden of maintaining the supply line. Moreover, concentrating the bulk of supplies at one port provided an excellent target for enemy air attack.

To move supplies and equipment forward from Pusan to the front the 2d Logistical Command utilized the Korean railroads as the chief means of transportation. But the Korean rail system left much to be desired. Its 3,500 miles of track are concentrated mostly in the western half of the peninsula, because the mountains prevent construction of lines in eastern Korea. Another complication is that the system's main trunk lines, one double track from Pusan to Seoul and a single track from Pusan to Ch'unch'on, have very few feeder lines. The forces in eastern Korea therefore had to truck supplies from the main lines over great distances.

The problems of rail support increased as the Eighth Army advanced northward and track mileage under its control lengthened. The rail system had suffered a good deal of damage in the fighting, and a shortage of rolling stock developed. Air and artillery bombardment had destroyed tracks and rolling stock, yards and repair shops, railroad bridges and tunnels, and a lack of enough skilled workers hindered the restoration of the damaged lines although the Eighth Army's engineers worked constantly at the job. The army's transportation section instituted a system of movements control to help overcome the shortage of rolling stock. It insisted that every car be fully loaded before shipping and unloaded quickly at its destination. The transportation section also obtained some rolling stock from Japanese sources and the United States, including locomotives. Despite all of these measures, a shortage of cars and motive power persisted throughout the course of the conflict.

As for the highway system of Korea, it was not built to support modern military operations. The roads are narrow, badly drained, and poorly surfaced. Snow and ice cover them in winter, and spring thaws and summer rains make them impassable. There were few laterals to connect with the main highways, and in many areas roads did not even exist or were merely ox-cart trails. Because supply agencies had to rely heavily on truck transportation, the Eighth Army's engineers spent a great deal of time and effort in improving and maintaining the existing roads and in constructing new roads.

Yet the tremendous improvements made by the engineers in South Korea's land transportation facilities were not enough to get the supplies to the combat troops. Trains and trucks brought the supplies from the ports to forward supply points. But from there to many sections of the front, food, clothing, ammunition, and other battlefield needs had to be hand-carried over the rugged terrain, a process that required a large number of men. Since combat troops could not be spared for such a task, the South Korean Government, at the request of the Eighth Army, organized the Korean Service Corps to carry supplies to the front lines. Laborers of this corps, using A-frames, daily toiled up the slopes of steep hills carrying needed supplies to the companies and platoons. They also assisted the front-line troops in building and improving fortifications.

As its principal means of communication in the Korean conflict, the Eighth Army used wire and very high frequency radio. Because the telephone and telegraph systems of South Korea had been seriously damaged by the war and were in a bad state of disrepair, the army's signal section built its own wire system extending from Pusan all the way to the front. The radio network supplemented the wire system to insure rapid and constant communication between all echelons of command. The ingenuity and hard work that went into the construction of the wire and radio networks produced in the end what was probably the finest communications system that any field army ever enjoyed.

Another problem posed for the Eighth Army was maintaining the supply of ammunition. When the conflict began, a great amount of ammunition left over from World War II was available for the support of the army. Transporting this ammunition to the front placed an additional burden on the inadequate rail and highway system of South Korea. As hostilities extended into the summer of 1951, ammunition levels in the depots began to approach the absolute minimum needed to sustain combat operations in Korea. The ammunition affected was shells for light and medium artillery and for mortars. A rationing program for normal combat operations was adopted to solve the problem. This program helped to relieve the strain on transportation facilities and insured that the army's guns would have all the ammunition necessary to stop an enemy drive or to support offensive operations.

Besides giving logistical support to the South Korean Army, the Eighth Army aided the civil population with relief supplies. From the very beginning of the conflict the Republic of Korea required civil assistance for its population. As the fighting spread over the whole country, the destruction of homes and fields, economic dislocations, and threats of disease and starvation imperiled the new nation. The South Korean Government did not have the means to cope with the problems of its tens of thousands of homeless refugees. Unless something was done, civil unrest would seriously impair the military effort of the U.N. forces in Korea. Thus civil relief became a military problem, at least while the fighting continued.

When the U.S. Army received responsibility for providing civil assistance to the Republic of Korea, it moved quickly. The Far East Command shipped food, clothing, and medicine from its supply depots to care for the refugees. Other relief items were purchased from Japanese sources. The Eighth Army organized the United Nations Civil Assistance Command (UNCACK) to provide relief. Working with the South Korean Government and U.N. representatives, this command supervised the organization of refugee camps, distributed food and clothing, and established medical facilities for the civil population. To prevent the spread of communicable diseases, more than three fourths of the population received inoculations against smallpox, typhoid, and typhus. Aircraft dusted cities with DDT to kill disease-bearing insects while teams dusted millions of South Koreans.

Thousands of children who had lost their families wandered with the refugees. Orphanages within the country rounded them up and cared for them, receiving aid from the Civil Assistance Command. In addition, thousands of American soldiers voluntarily contributed money to support homes for them. Many units of the Eighth Army "adopted" orphanages, supporting them with money, clothing, food, and other necessities.

Another objective of the civil relief mission in Korea was to assist the country in rebuilding its economy. The Civil Assistance Command helped to rebuild and expand the agricultural economy by providing technical guidance and material aid. At the same time the South Koreans were helped and encouraged to build factories for the production of war matériel and consumer goods, and the nation's government took steps to reduce inflation. This economic program was reinforced by the Eighth Army's employment of thousands of Korean workers and the rebuilding and improvement of the railroads, highways, ports, and airfields of the country.

Another problem bristling with difficulties arose from the large number of enemy soldiers held by the Eighth Army. When the North Korean forces collapsed near the end of 1950, the Eighth Army had well over 100,000 prisoners of war on its hands. These prisoners were held on the island of Koje-do, situated thirty miles southwest of Pusan. The camp consisted of four barbed wire enclosures each subdivided into eight compounds, with each compound capable of holding 6,000 prisoners.

The camp administration carried out the principles of the Geneva Convention of 1949 regarding prisoners of war. Guards re-

215

ceived instructions in these principles, and representatives of the International Red Cross inspected the compounds frequently. The captives were permitted to engage in athletics, and classes of instruction in a great variety of subjects were offered to those who wished to attend.

Camp authorities also instituted a screening program to separate South Korean civilians from the real prisoners of war. These civilians had been forced to fight or to work as laborers in the North Korean Army when it overran the Republic of Korea during the first months of the war. As a result of the screening program 38,000 captives were reclassified as civilians during November and December 1951. Then, in January 1952, the camp commander began a second screening cycle to correct mistakes made in the first one. Communist leaders within the compounds resisted this screening because it meant that they would lose control over the anticommunist prisoners and that the guards could keep a closer watch over antagonistic groups.

During the early months of the camp's operation disorders occurred often, but rioting did not break out until late in 1951. Evidently a core of tough communists had been organized in each compound with the objective of seizing control over the anticommunists among the prisoners. Gangs of thugs cowed those who would not conform, and kangaroo courts sentenced leaders of the opposition to death. This attempt to seize control of the captives within each compound led to factional strife and a number of deaths.

Violent opposition to screening began in early 1952, when the inmates of Compound 62 attacked a battalion of troops from the U.S. 27th Infantry Regiment. The battalion had entered the compound to keep order while the Republic of Korea screen-ing committee performed its duties. The prisoners attacked the Americans with rocks, pick handles, homemade knives and axes, tent poles, and barbed wire flails. The soldiers threw concussion grenades to stop the attack, but the mob continued to move forward. The American commander ordered his troops to fire, and the prisoners were forced back. When the melee ceased, 200 inmates of the compound were casualties and one American had been killed and thirty-eight wounded.

As a result of the riot the guard strength was increased and a new screening and segregation program instituted. The new program called for separation of those prisoners and civilian internees who desired repatriation from those who did not and for construction of new prisoner of war camps on the mainland and the island of Cheju-do.

As the new screening program began, in April 1952, it met with increasing hostility from the communist prisoners. Mass meetings, flag raisings, and other acts of defiance took place. The climax came in May when the prisoners seized the commander of the prisoner of war camp. General Van Fleet immediately moved reinforcements to the island, including flame-throwing tanks. Upon release of the camp's head, Brig. Gen. Haydon L. Boatner took over command and proceeded to bring the situation under control. General Boatner had all civilian residents of the island moved off, reorganized the staff, and ordered his guards to enter forcibly any compound displaying slogans or flying North Korean flags. Engineers began rebuilding the compounds to reduce their capacity to 500 men, and the army commander sent the 187th Airborne Regiment to reinforce the guard strength of the camp.

The communist leaders prepared to fight against any removal of the prisoners. They

216

secretly fashioned weapons, filling crude grenades with hoarded cooking gasoline. The inmates of one compound dug a waist-deep trench before the main gate on the assumption that the guards would enter there.

On 10 June the camp commander proceeded to move the prisoners to the new compounds. The leader of Compound 76, where the trench had been dug, was ordered to form his men into groups of 150 in preparation for the move. He failed to do so, and General Boatner ordered the commander of the 187th to move two battalions into the compound. The troops did not enter by the main gate. Instead engineers cut through the barbed wire in rear of the compound while tanks patrolled outside of the enclosure. Then the troops, wearing gas masks, advanced through the cut in the wire and threw tear gas grenades into the unruly mob. The grenades ignited gasoline hidden in the compound, and the inmates broke before the American troops. Some locked themselves in the barracks of the enclosure while others jumped into the ditch near the main gate. The troops began a methodical job of cleaning out the barracks and ditch, herding the captives toward the center of the compound. In one and a half hours it was all over. Nearly 6,000 North Koreans squatted in the center of the enclosure while the compound's buildings went up in flames. Over 150 inmates were killed and injured; the Americans had one killed and thirteen wounded. Shortly afterward the prisoners were moved to the new compound while their leader was led off to solitary confinement.

With the collapse of the prisoners' revolt in Compound 76, the remainder of the screening program was carried out with relatively little difficulty. The noncommunist prisoners were separated from the communists, and the latter moved into the 500-man compounds. Incidents on the island continued, but guards used tear gas to stop demonstrations and riots and to maintain order and discipline among the unruly inmates.

SECTION 7

12 November 1951–30 June 1952

STATION GYPSY, near Hwach'on. Operations van from which programs were broadcast (left) contained two short-wave receivers, two dual-speed turntables, an amplifier for live broadcasts, a transmitter, console, microphone, tape recorder, and library of over 35,000 song hits; administrative van is on the right.

378TH ENGINEER COMBAT BATTALION constructing a treadway bridge across the Pukhan River, ROK 6th Division sector of IX Corps area, November 1951.

Patton Tank on the Main Supply Route, 3d Division sector, I Corps area, 17 November 1951.

WINTRY WASHDAY in the 24th Division area, 24 November.

8-INCH HOWITZER in action, 25th Division area.

CLEARING SLUSH from a 24th Division landing strip.

GUARD DUTY. Snow-covered vehicle is a halftrack, Quad .50.

VICE-PRESIDENT ALBEN W. BARKLEY, right foreground, is welcomed to the 24th Division area by the Colombian Battalion Commander; Maj. Gen. Blackshear M. Bryan, Commanding General, 24th Division, is at right.

"Wish those guys at the peace conference would hurry it up, my feet are gettin' cold."

WET AND CHILLED, cavalrymen huddle around a small can of burning gasoline.

LITTER BEARERS OF THE 7TH DIVISION, moving cautiously over ice and snow, bring in a wounded man.

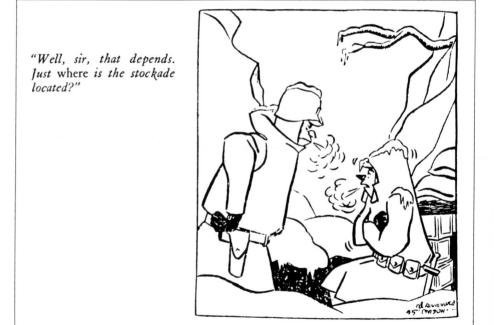

"Well, sir, that depends. Just where is the stockade located?"

ENEMY PRISONER, captured by a 7th Division soldier, is on his way south for the winter.

SELF-PROPELLED 155-MM. GUN lights up the night in the 25th Division area, 26 November.

Flying Boxcar C-119 Disgorging Mail for APO 24, Ch'unch'on.

PATTON TANKS PINCH-HITTING FOR MAIL TRUCKS carry Christmas mail to front-line troops.

ROLLS OF BARBED WIRE AND MAIL on the way up to Company E, 21st Infantry.

RIDGERUNNER, so called because of its maneuverability on the roadway above running along the ridge line. The tank shown above is credited with having destroyed eighteen enemy bunkers in one afternoon.

INSULATED CONTAINERS OF HOT FOOD being carried up to hilltop positions, 24th Division area.

ENEMY BUNKER AND CONNECTING TRENCH, Hill 770.

ENEMY KITCHEN on Hill 770 near Kumsong.

TANK COMMANDER crouching behind the turret after giving the order to fire.

CABLE CAR, built by 3d Engineer Construction Battalion. Starting point is at foot of Hill 770, left; the car nears the platform at the top of the hill, below. Engine from a discarded ¾-ton truck supplied power for the car, which traversed a distance of 1,530 feet from bottom to top. At several stages of its journey the car dangled as much as 200 feet off the ground.

COMPANY E, 21ST INFANTRY, preparing for a long winter, near Kumsong. Koreans help with construction of bunker, right. Assistant squad leaders attend a class on the use and operation of grenade adapters, below.

Some troops see Santa.

Some troops do not.

"Now I don't mind if y' live here, but ya gotta stop bringin' yer friends around fer them parties late at night!"

Now I lay me down to sleep. . . .

REPLACEMENTS for the 1st Marine Division disembarking from an LST.

L-20 Preparing To Take Off. Seated in front with the pilot is Maj. Gen. Williston B. Palmer, Commanding General, X Corps.

White-Clad Reconnaissance Patrol from 2d Division moving out, 1 January 1952.

New Year's Day Dinner on its way up to Company L, 21st Infantry, near Kumsong.

"Sure ain't hard to spot the music lovers."

CELEBRATING NEW YEAR'S DAY

PLOTTING CORRECTIONS ON A MAP in the fire control hut before the next heavy mortar rounds are fired, west of Ch'orwon, 4 January.

SERVING A HOT MEAL to the 179th Infantry Regiment, 45th Division, along a mountainside. The 45th Division arrived in Korea during the third week of December.

JANUARY 1952. In this month the Eighth Army opened a sustained artillery-air campaign against enemy positions.

Destroying an Old Enemy Bunker With TNT, near Kumsong, 11 January.

40th Division Infantrymen preparing to debark at Inch'on harbor, January 1952. The 40th Division was assigned to the IX Corps to relieve the 24th Division.

24TH DIVISION TROOPS aboard the USS *George Clymer* headed for Japan.

COFFEE BREAK for 40th Division men on their way to the front lines two days after arriving in Korea.

UNCACK Representative Presenting a Jeep-Type Fire Engine to a Korean public safety officer, Taejon, October 1952.

Partially Constructed Family Housing Units, Taegu, July 1952.

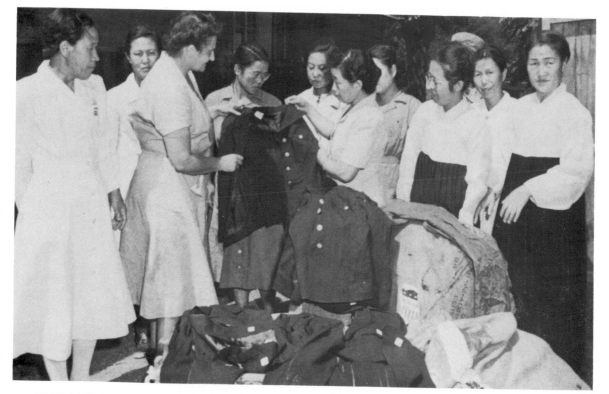

UNCACK Chief Nurse With Korean Women examining American women's uniforms donated to hospitals, August 1952.

The United Nations Civil Assistance Command (UNCACK), in providing relief for the civil population of South Korea, distributed food and clothing, reconstructed communities, and furnished medical facilities.

Cement Donated by UNCACK was used to make well casings and pipe, July 1952.

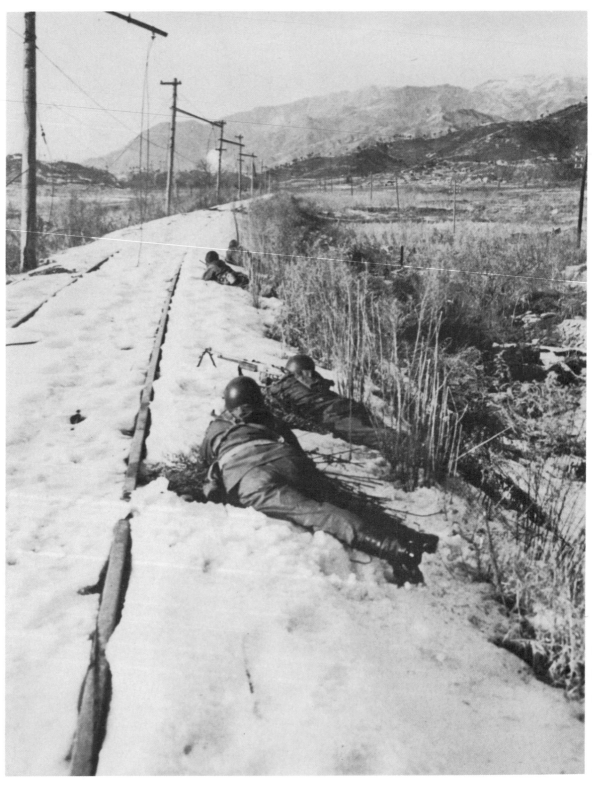

FRENCH BATTALION TROOPS ON MANEUVERS, shown in positions along the electric railroad track at Kumgong-ni.

INSTALLING A FIELD TELEPHONE at the 160th Infantry regimental command post.

LEAVING WARMING TENTS to carry out a fire mission. The men above are from Battery B, 37th Field Artillery Battalion.

Medic Treating Injured 2d Division Infantryman, 14 February 1952, while a wounded ROK soldier is helped up the steep bank to await his turn.

U.N. POW Camp, Koje-do. Korean village, foreground, borders the camp.

All-Prisoner Cast of a play staged for the entertainment of the POW camp, Koje-do, March 1952.

TAKING TIME OUT for coffee and doughnuts, 37th Field Artillery Battalion command post.

SEARCHLIGHT IN POSITION, west of Ch'orwon. This searchlight is mounted on the bed of a converted 2½-ton truck.

SAVING AN AIRMAN

FIRING ROCKETS FROM A PT BOAT in a harassing attack against the east coast of North Korea. The boat is manned by ROK Navy men.

Low-Level Air Attack on enemy supply center at Suan, thirty-five miles southeast of P'yong-yang. Note tank of napalm just released from the left wing of the F-80.

"Hey, sarge, it must be spring—your sakura's bloomin'!"

PLATOON LEADER BRIEFING HIS MEN before leaving on a reconnaissance patrol, June 1952.

CONFERENCE IN THE RAIN, June 1952. General Van Fleet, Eighth Army commander, is on the left; next to him is Brig. Gen. Joseph P. Cleland, Commanding General, 40th Division; Maj. Gen. Willard G. Wyman, Commanding General, IX Corps, is at right.

Welcome home.

1 JULY 1952–27 JULY 1953

CHAPTER IX

Outpost Battles

1 July–31 December 1952

Deadlock continued as the Korean conflict went into its third year in late June 1952. Since November 1951 the battle front had been relative stable, both sides having settled down to an active defense of their positions. In the following winter and spring the fighting dwindled to patrol clashes, raids, and small-scale attacks, but the enemy grew more aggressive in May 1952 and action along the entire front increased. Enemy attempts to seize key outposts and terrain guarding the approaches to the Eighth Army's main positions sparked frequent and intense fire fights during the summer and fall of 1952. The army successfully defended these positions, breaking up the enemy's attacks and killing thousands of Chinese and North Koreans.

July began with a series of small-scale attacks by both sides. In the Eighth Army's western sector the U.S. I Corps, under its new commander, Maj. Gen. Paul W. Kendall, conducted a number of raids on Chinese fortifications opposite the corps' front. On the first day of the month, infantrymen from the ROK 1st Division raided enemy positions overlooking the Imjin River. In the fight that followed the ROK troops killed 112 Chinese before returning to the division's lines. Two days later, on 3 July, the marines, on the corps' left wing, struck at a Chinese battalion. Supported by mor-

tar and artillery fire, two companies from the 7th Marine Regiment swept into the enemy positions to inflict 200 casualties on the surprised Chinese before retiring. The corps handed out more punishment when a tank-infantry team from General Ruffner's U.S. 45th Division attacked a hill mass northwest of Ch'orwon. The tankers and infantrymen returned to their lines after killing seventy-nine of the enemy on the hill.

Light action marked the fighting on the remainder of the front. In General Wyman's U.S. IX Corps, troops from Maj. Gen. Wayne C. Smith's U.S. 7th Division raided an enemy-held hill ten miles south of P'yonggang on 3 July. The raiding infantrymen wiped out the forty-five Chinese defenders and destroyed enemy fortifications before returning to their lines. The ROK 9th Division followed up this raid with two of their own against enemy positions, killing sixty Chinese and destroying bunkers, trenches, and gun emplacements. In the ROK II Corps area South Korean infantrymen struck enemy positions northeast of Kumhwa to kill sixty-five Chinese. In the ROK I Corps sector North Korean troops unsuccessfully attacked an observation post for naval gunfire on the enemy's Nam River communications line. The enemy lost an estimated 600 men in this attempt.

Torrential rains in the last week of July and the first week of August restricted activity along the front, but periods of clear weather brought renewed attacks by both sides. In the U.S. I Corps zone Maj. Gen. James C. Fry, the U.S. 2d Division commander, sent two reinforced companies against Hill 266 during the night of 31 July–1 August. Determined to regain the height that had been lost in July, the infantrymen stormed up the slopes and drove the Chinese out. Quickly digging in and organizing their position, the 2d Division troops awaited the inevitable counterattack. It came the following night, but massed division artillery and small arms fire broke up the Chinese assault. Enemy attacks later in the month met with no success, and the hill remained in the hands of the 2d Division.

Heavy rains again drenched Korea in the latter part of August to bring the fighting to a near halt. Then, as September began, the skies cleared and the enemy renewed his assaults on the Eighth Army's outpost positions. These attacks were accompanied by an increasing amount of mortar and artillery fire support.

For quite some time the enemy had gradually been increasing the volume of mortar and artillery fire used in support of his attacks. In September an all-time high of 45,000 rounds fell on the army's front in one day. Despite the enormous effort exerted by the Fifth Air Force and the naval air arm to sever the enemy's supply lines the Chinese and North Koreans kept their front-line troops supplied and even managed to accumulate a reserve stock of ammunition and supplies.

Various sectors of the Eighth Army's line came under enemy attack in September. After unsuccessfully assaulting an outpost that the marines had seized and established the previous month, the Chinese shifted their efforts to the U.S. I Corps' right wing. On the night of 18 September, after their artillery had smothered Hill 266 in the U.S. 2d Division sector with 1,000 shells, an estimated two enemy companies, reinforced with tanks, swarmed up the slopes and rapidly overran the crest. The Americans withdrew 400 yards and established new positions, then counterattacked. But the heavy and accurate Chinese artillery fire prevented the assaulting troops from making any headway. On the evening of 20 September another American counterattack formed and began to envelop the hill. After slow progress through heavy enemy fire the attacking companies, reinforced by a platoon of tanks, made a co-ordinated assault that carried them to the crest. The Chinese fell back as the attacking infantrymen swept over the hilltop and secured the position.

In the central sector of the Eighth Army line, the enemy struck at two separate points in the front of the ROK II Corps' Capital Division. On the division's left flank the Chinese overran an outpost position to threaten the main line of resistance while another outpost on the division's right fell to enemy assaults. Both were soon retaken by the South Korean infantrymen.

In the eastern sector of the front North Koreans attacked main line of resistance positions on the right wing of the U.S. X Corps on the night of 21–22 September. While the U.S. 45th Division was in the process of relieving the ROK 8th Division, elements of two enemy battalions overran the western slope and crest of a hill serving as part of the ROK division's main line. Driving one company back about 1,000 yards, the attacking enemy then swung to the west to widen the penetration. But the defending South Koreans on the left of the penetration held firm and halted the North

Korean attack. The next morning, 22 September, an infantry company from the ROK 8th Division, supported by tanks from the 45th Division's 245th Tank Battalion, managed to regain part of the hill. At noon of the same day, after artillery fire and air strikes had covered the penetration, elements of the ROK 8th's reserve regiment counterattacked and drove the enemy back. By nightfall the main line of resistance had been restored and all enemy troops driven out. During the next two days the North Koreans made several weak efforts to penetrate the division's main line without success. Meanwhile the 45th Division continued its relief of the 8th, completing it on 26 September.

While the troops of the Eighth Army defended their outposts and main battle positions against local enemy assaults, the air war over Korea intensified during the summer of 1952. Aircraft from the Fifth Air Force and the Far East Bomber Command, Marine aircraft, and Navy carrier-based planes struck at supply centers, troop concentrations, power plants, factories, and rail and road networks. In addition to striking deep into enemy territory, air units rendered valuable assistance to front-line troops. Enemy bunkers, trenches, gun positions, and communication lines were bombed or seared with napalm. On 29 August the Fifth Air Force carried out the largest air raid of the Korean conflict. Hundreds of Air Force, Marine, and Navy planes accompanied by aircraft from Australia and the United Kingdom raided P'yongyang, the North Korean capital. In this massive strike, supply installations, repair shops, troop concentrations, military headquarters, and a host of other targets were destroyed or badly damaged.

An increasing number of enemy jet interceptors rose to challenge Fifth Air Force Sabrejets during the summer. But the superiority of American pilots was clearly demonstrated by the number of enemy aircraft destroyed in aerial combat. During the month of September alone, pilots from the Fifth Air Force shot down sixty-four MIG-15's at a cost of seven Sabrejets.

The Navy maintained its blockade of both coasts of North Korea. On the east coast, warships of the U.S. Seventh Fleet continued to bombard the enemy port of Wonsan. Ships from the fleet also continued to provide gunfire support to friendly forces near the east coast of the peninsula. On the Korean west coast the U.N. fleet helped protect islands off the North Korean coast and assisted guerrilla units to recapture an island that had been seized by an enemy force.

The rising tide of enemy attacks that began in May culminated in a series of assaults in October that produced some of the heaviest fighting in more than a year. Battles raged on many sections of the front as Chinese and North Korean units, sometimes employing their familiar human-sea tactics, tried to penetrate the Eighth Army's main line of resistance or to seize dominating terrain. The heaviest fighting centered around two key heights, Hills 281 and 395, northwest of Ch'orwon. Capture of these strategic positions, astride the U.S. I Corps–U.S. IX Corps boundary, would give the Chinese control of the lateral roads behind the corps' lines and threaten the main supply route to Ch'orwon.

To herald the opening of their attacks the Chinese unleashed the largest volume of mortar and artillery fire received by the Eighth Army since the fighting began. On one day, 7 October, more than 93,000 rounds fell on U.N. positions along the front. The Eighth Army estimated that during these attacks the enemy's daily expenditure of artillery and mortar ammunition doubled to more than 24,000 rounds.

The Chinese began a co-ordinated attack against both hills on the evening of 6 October after a daylong artillery bombardment of the objectives. Two enemy companies struck Hill 281, the eastern anchor of the I Corps line. The U.S. 2d Division's French Battalion, defending the height, repelled this assault, but the Chinese added two more companies to the attacking force, reformed, and attacked again. The gallant French would not yield, and as the battle progressed the Chinese continued to build up their attacking strength. By dawn, they had an entire regiment hammering away vainly at the French. Finally, with hundreds of their dead and wounded strewn about the besieged position, the Chinese broke off the attack and withdrew. They kept up pressure against the French-held hill for the next few days, but on 12 October abandoned further attempts to capture it.

The main enemy attack in the meantime struck Hill 395, guarding the U.S. IX Corps left flank. The Chinese hurled an estimated two battalions against the height in co-ordination with the attack on Hill 281. Elements of the ROK 9th Division, defending the hill, held their positions until the following afternoon, 7 October, when the enemy threw in additional battalions and forced the South Koreans to withdraw. A counterattack restored the lost ground, but the enemy renewed his assault in regimental strength the next day and again forced the ROK troops to withdraw. They established a new defense line south of the lost positions and then began to counterattack. Assisted by numerous air strikes and the massed corps artillery, the South Korean infantrymen managed after two days of heavy fighting to fight their way to the crest of the hill and drive the Chinese back.

An enemy battalion then attempted to push the infantrymen back, but the defenders, backed up by artillery fire, stopped the Chinese short of their goal.

To relieve the pressure against Hill 395 a battalion from the ROK 9th Division, supported by a company-sized tank-infantry team, seized high ground several hundred yards north of the hill. Securing this newly won terrain, the battalion continued to advance northward and by 15 October had secured two screening positions 1,000 yards north of Hill 395. With the South Koreans now in firm control of the disputed ground the enemy gave up further efforts to penetrate the IX Corps left flank. After the battle was all over, the 9th Division reported that the major part of a Chinese reserve division from the *38th Chinese Communist Army* had been destroyed. Over 2,000 Chinese dead were counted on the slopes of Hills 281 and 395 in the ten-day battle.

The Eighth Army countered enemy aggressiveness by making several attacks during the middle of the month. The primary aim of these attacks was to strengthen the defense of Kumhwa, the right leg of the Iron Triangle and the hub of an important road net. Two dominating hill masses, Hills 500 and 598, about four miles north of the city were the objectives of the IX Corps' U.S. 7th and ROK 2d Divisions. The attack began on the morning of 14 October when two battalions from the 7th Division's 31st Regiment executed a double envelopment of Hill 598 from the south and southeast. Advancing under heavy enemy fire, the battalions succeeded in driving the enemy from the hill after six hours of intense fighting. The Chinese counterattacked that night and forced the Americans off the height.

The next morning, 15 October, the infantrymen of the 31st again attacked. Moving silently and swiftly through the morning mists they went up the slopes of Hill 598 and ejected the enemy from the crest. Two smaller heights that lay a short distance from the main objective also fell to the attacking troops. The Chinese then retaliated by throwing two battalions against the hill in an effort to dislodge the Americans. The enemy attack failed. Three days later, on 18 October, the American infantrymen advanced another 1,000 yards deeper into enemy territory and seized key terrain to protect Hill 598 from the north. But counterattacking Chinese battalions forced the troops of the 31st to pull back to the main hill mass. Further enemy attempts to regain Hill 598 failed until 30 October. At that time, three days after the ROK 2d Division had taken over the height from the U.S. 7th Division, an enemy regiment stormed up the slopes and drove out the South Korean defenders. Successive counterattacks by the 2d failed to regain the hill.

While the 7th Division had been fighting for Hill 598, a battalion from the ROK 2d Division streamed up Hill 500 and seized the crest against light enemy opposition. The usual enemy counterattack followed, and for a week the position changed hands repeatedly. Near the end of October the ROK troops finally managed to seize and hold the height.

Meanwhile more fighting broke out in the ROK II Corps' sector. Two Chinese companies attacked hilltop positions near the left flank of the ROK Capital Division on the night of 6 October. The South Koreans made a determined stand and prevented the enemy from making any penetration of the main battle line. About 500 yards east of these positions the enemy also struck with two companies and seized an outpost guarding the division's center. The following morning ROK troops counter-attacked and managed to reach positions 300 yards from the crest. The Chinese prevented any further advance, and as October ended the enemy still remained in possession of the hilltop.

Fighting along the remainder of the Eighth Army front consisted of patrol clashes and light raids by the enemy. Harassing attacks occurred on the U.S. I Corps' front against the 1st Marine Division when the Chinese attacked several outposts without success.

With the coming of winter weather in November, enemy aggressiveness began to decline. Although the Chinese kept pressure on the central front, the severe defeat inflicted on them by the IX Corps in October and the adverse weather evidently dampened their desire to conduct further large-scale attacks against the Eighth Army's battle line. For the remainder of the year fighting diminished in intensity as both sides prepared to meet the rigors of the Korean winter.

Although most of the front remained relatively quiet, in the U.S. I Corps sector the enemy tried to penetrate a part of the 1st British Commonwealth Division's front line on 19 November. The British threw back the attack after killing over a hundred Chinese. Fighting again flared up in the corps area when the ROK 1st Division beat back Chinese attempts to overrun outposts on the Imjin River line in December. The enemy then tried to seize key terrain in front of the U.S. 2d Division. In a short but intense battle the Americans killed 111 of the enemy and captured four prisoners. The Chinese then withdrew their attacking force.

Enemy attacks on the central front during the last two months of the year resulted in several brief but bitter fights. On the IX

Corps left wing an enemy battalion seized an outpost in front of the U.S. 3d Division's lines on 6 November. Shortly after this success the Chinese made an attempt to break through the defenses of the U.S. 7th Division's Ethiopian Battalion. After a brief fire fight the enemy withdrew leaving 131 of his dead around the Ethiopians' positions.

On the eastern front an enemy force struck several positions in the U.S. X Corps center. The U.S. 40th Division quickly broke up these assaults, killing 152 of the enemy and capturing seven. Farther east, in the ROK I Corps sector, two North Korean battalions made a minor penetration of the ROK 5th Division's lines. Counterattacking South Korean infantrymen ejected the enemy and restored the positions.

As ground fighting slowed to a near halt during December, General Van Fleet made several changes in his battle line. To strengthen the Kumhwa–Ch'orwon sector of the Iron Triangle, the army commander increased the number of front-line divisions in the IX Corps. The front of the ROK 9th Division, on the corps' right flank, was narrowed and the left boundary of the ROK II Corps shifted several miles to the east. The ROK Capital Division then filled in the resulting gap. One other change occurred in the IX Corps when the ROK 2d Division relieved the U.S. 3d Division on the corps' left flank. Lt. Gen. Reuben E. Jenkins, who had taken over command of the IX Corps from General Wyman in August, now had three ROK divisions and one U.S. division, the 25th, defending his front.

In the western sector of the army's battle line, the U.S. 7th Division relieved the U.S. 2d Division on the U.S. I Corps' right flank. On the eastern front a newly created South Korean division, the ROK 12th, entered combat for the first time, replacing the U.S.

45th Division on the right flank of the U.S. X Corps.

At the year's end General Van Fleet had sixteen divisions manning the Eighth Army's battle line. Included in this number were one U.S. Marine, one British Commonwealth, eleven South Korean, and three U.S. Army divisions. Contingents of troops from other United Nations countries reinforced the American divisions, and a Korean Marine regiment became an important adjunct to the 1st Marine Division. The army commander also had four divisions available as reserve forces—one South Korean and three American.

By giving the South Koreans responsibility for defending nearly 75 percent of the Eighth Army's front General Van Fleet indicated that he had confidence in the ability of the revitalized ROK Army to hold its own against large-scale enemy attacks. It was evident that the South Korean Army, trained and equipped by the U.S. Army, was now a fighting force capable of effective defense.

For over a year now a stalemate had existed in the Korean conflict. Both sides had constructed defense lines so powerful that their reduction could be accomplished only at a prohibitive cost. This had limited the Eighth Army's offensive operations during 1952 to small-scale attacks to prevent the enemy from holding terrain features close to the army's main line of resistance and raids to hamper the enemy's build-up of defensive positions.

During the year the Eighth Army also conducted a vigorous defense of its outpost positions. These outposts, located on high ground to screen the army's main line of resistance, became the objective of frequent enemy attack, particularly in the latter half of the year. The Eighth Army threw back the great majority of these assaults and inflicted thousands of casualties on the enemy. Positions that did fall, owing to the weight of enemy numbers, were quickly restored by counterattacking Eighth Army infantrymen. Occasionally an outpost position had to be abandoned when it became clear that the enemy intended to seize the position at any cost. In this case the outpost lost its usefulness as the price of holding it or retaking it outweighed its tactical value in delaying enemy attacks on the main line of resistance.

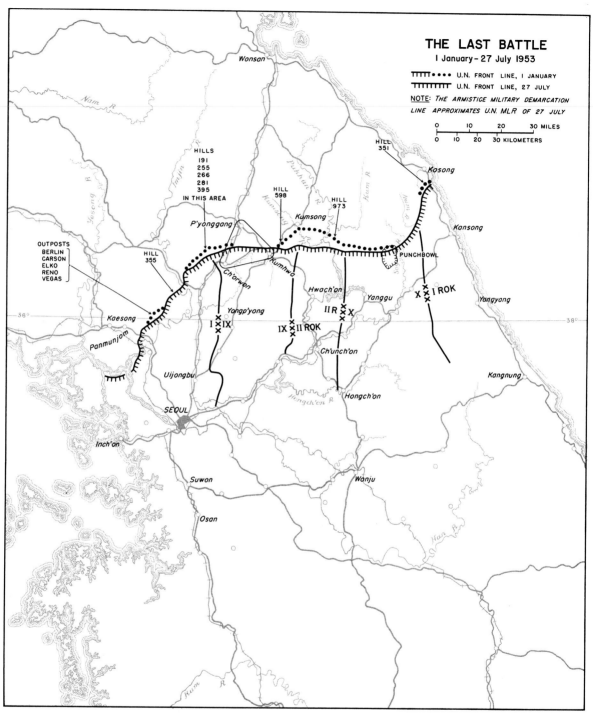

THE LAST BATTLE
1 January – 27 July 1953

U.N. FRONT LINE, 1 JANUARY
U.N. FRONT LINE, 27 JULY
NOTE: THE ARMISTICE MILITARY DEMARCATION
LINE APPROXIMATES U.N. MLR OF 27 JULY

0   10   20   30 MILES
0   10   20   30 KILOMETERS

Wonsan

Nam R.

HILL
351

Kosong

HILLS
191
255
266
281
395
IN THIS AREA

HILL
598

HILL
973

P'yonggang

Kumsong

Kansong

PUNCHBOWL

OUTPOSTS
BERLIN
CARSON
ELKO
RENO
VEGAS

HILL
355

Ch'orwon

Kumhwa

Hwach'on

Yanggu

X X X I ROK

Yangyang

38°   38°

Kaesong

Yongp'yong

II R X X

Panmunjom

I X IX

IX X II ROK

Ch'unch'on

Kangnung

Uijongbu

Hongch'on R.

Hongch'on

SEOUL

Inch'on

Suwon

Wanju

Osan

Han R.

Ham   R.

MAP 7

J.R. Crowley

276

CHAPTER X

The Last Battle

1 January–27 July 1953

As the year 1953 began, activity along the entire front subsided. Patrolling and small-scale harassing attacks characterized the fighting during the winter months of the new year. Then, as spring began, the enemy renewed his assaults upon the Eighth Army's outpost line, attempting to seize terrain that overlooked the army's main line of resistance. These attacks increased in frequency and intensity until, in July, they approached the scale of the enemy's heavy attacks of May 1951.

During January 1953 General Van Fleet continued to make changes in the Eighth Army's line. In the right-wing corps, he replaced the veteran ROK 5th Division with the newly activated 15th. In the left-wing corps, the U.S. 2d Division relieved the 1st British Commonwealth Division, the first time the latter unit had been out of combat for nearly eighteen months. In the IX Corps, in the Eighth Army's center, the U.S. 3d Division took over the sector held by the U.S. 25th Division, while in X Corps the U.S. 45th relieved the U.S. 40th Division. After these changes the army commander had twelve South Korean and eight U.N. divisions to defend the army front. The thousands of service and security troops that supported the combat divisions brought the army's total strength to nearly 768,000 men.

To oppose the Eighth Army's twenty divisions the enemy disposed a formidable array of strength along his front. Seven Chinese armies and two North Korean corps, totaling about 270,000 troops, manned the enemy defense line. Another eleven Chinese armies and North Korean corps with an estimated strength of 531,000 remained in reserve. With service and security forces, the total enemy strength in Korea amounted to more than a million men.

The enemy employed his forces along a battle line that roughly paralleled that of the Eighth Army. The Chinese occupied about three fourths of this line; their armies extended from the Korean west coast eastward to the Kum River. East of the river the North Koreans manned the remainder of the line to the Sea of Japan—a sector, incidentally, where there was little likelihood of a main U.N. thrust. Although a manpower shortage probably explains this division of responsibility, it is also possible that the Chinese questioned the fighting ability of their allies.

Other than a few patrol clashes, little fighting occurred during January and February. Only in the sector of the ROK 12th Division did the enemy make any serious attempts to penetrate the army's main line of resistance, and these failed. Meanwhile, the Eighth Army carried out a number of raids on enemy positions. Supported by air strikes and accurate artillery fire, raiding parties from all five corps struck hard at Chinese and North Korean positions to kill or capture enemy soldiers and destroy emplacements and fortifications.

During February the command of the Eighth Army changed hands. General Van Fleet, after nearly two years as the Eighth Army's leader, turned over his command to Lt. Gen. Maxwell D. Taylor and returned to the United States for retirement.

As March began the enemy increased his attacks on the army's outpost line, evidently in retaliation for the U.N. raids of January and February. The U.S. I Corps bore the brunt of these attacks. On the first day of March an enemy battalion assaulted main line of resistance positions on Hill 355, held by elements of the U.S. 2d Division. Although part of the enemy force managed to reach the foxholes and trenches of the defenders the attack was beaten off. The Chinese hit the hill again on 17 March with a battalion. Attacking in two elements from the north and northeast, the Chinese breached the protective mine fields and wire and drove into the trenches on the crest. The center of the line gave way, but two platoons that had been previously placed in blocking positions moved up to contain the penetration. Meanwhile, on the crest and forward slope of the hill the fighting was heavy. At dawn an infantry company arrived to reinforce the troops on the hilltop and the Chinese began withdrawing. As they pulled back, U.N. artillery fire hit their routes of withdrawal and inflicted further casualties.

The Chinese again struck at the U.S. I Corps during the final week of the month. On the evening of 23 March an enemy regiment assaulted Hills 266, 255, and 191,

outposts of the U.S. 7th Division. Defended by the division's Colombian Battalion, Hill 266 was the target of the main enemy effort. A Chinese battalion supported by artillery and mortar fire drove into positions on the western slope of the hill at 2100. The Colombians on the hill received reinforcements amounting to a company, but this was not enough to withstand the enemy assault and the defenders fell back to positions on the southeastern slope of the height. The following morning, 24 March, a battalion from the 7th Division counterattacked and managed to gain the crest of the hill and engage the Chinese in trenches and bunkers. The struggle continued throughout the morning with both sides supported by heavy artillery fire. The Chinese stubbornly fought to retain their positions, and the Americans broke off their attack, pulling back to the southern slope. Early the next day another American counterattack failed, and the Chinese still held the crest of Hill 266.

Concurrently with the attack on Hill 266 two enemy battalions hit Hills 255 and 191. The battle on Hill 191 was short. As the Chinese companies advanced up the slopes the Americans called for and received reinforcements. After a brief fire fight with the defenders, the Chinese broke contact and withdrew. Over on Hill 255 the Chinese were more successful. Supported by tanks and by artillery and mortar fire the Chinese forced the defenders to withdraw 700 yards. Shortly after midnight two companies from the 7th Division counterattacked up Hill 255 and drove the enemy off the crest.

Although the Chinese had gained their chief objective, Hill 266, the price was high. The 7th Division reported that the battles on the three hills cost the enemy 750 casualties.

278

While the battle seesawed about the outposts in the 7th Division sector, the enemy prepared for another attack farther to the west in the I Corps sector. Early in the evening of 26 March several outposts of the 1st Marine Regiment received diversionary attacks by small enemy forces. Then the enemy struck three nearby outposts in regimental strength. Overrunning two of the three positions quickly, the Chinese advanced toward the main line of resistance. But an American blocking force, placed between the Chinese line of advance and the main line of resistance, intercepted the enemy regiment. After a vain, all-night effort to get by this obstacle the Chinese withdrew. Later in the morning of 27 March a marine battalion counterattacked and recaptured one of the lost outposts. The rest of the day and all through the following night the marines pressed their attack forward. By morning of the next day, 28 March, they took the remaining outpost, but shortly afterward a Chinese counterthrust drove the Americans back 400 yards. In the afternoon the marines again regained the outpost. Reinforcing and digging in, they awaited the next onslaught. It came that night when a Chinese battalion attacked. More marine reinforcements were poured in while corps and division artillery fire isolated the battlefield and prevented the Chinese from increasing the size of their attacking force. By the next morning the enemy had made no more headway and withdrew.

Friendly and enemy patrols kept busy in the I Corps sector. The Chinese, apparently sensitive to the activities of the corps' patrols and raiding parties, began to establish ambushes. One patrol of thirty-four men from the U.S. 7th Division fell into a trap set by the enemy on 9 March. Surrounded by some sixty Chinese the whole patrol became casualties: twenty men were killed, twelve wounded, and two missing. On another occasion a thirty-four-man patrol from the U.S. 2d Division ran head on into two Chinese companies. The patrol called for and received reinforcements, and the resulting engagement lasted until the next morning when the enemy broke contact and withdrew. The Americans suffered a total of sixty-three casualties in this fight, twelve of them killed, forty-three wounded, and five missing. Two platoons from the Colombian Battalion, raiding enemy positions on the morning of 10 March, engaged the Chinese in a short but intense fire fight. Forced to withdraw under heavy enemy artillery fire, the Colombians lost nineteen men killed, forty-four wounded, and eight missing.

After the flare-up of fighting in late March, activity along the battle front again settled into routine patrolling and small-scale harassing attacks. The calm persisted throughout April, interrupted only by Eighth Army raids on the enemy's outpost and main line of resistance positions. But as April ended, and the armistice negotiations at Panmunjom approached a decisive stage, there were signs that the enemy intended to increase the size and frequency of his attacks. Troop movements indicated that he was shifting his forces from the northern coastal areas and concentrating them in more forward areas. His artillery and armor were being positioned in depth and his troops realigned on the front and in the rear. An increasing number of contacts between Eighth Army and enemy patrols showed considerable tightening of the enemy counterreconnaissance screen.

Then, in the final week of May, the Chinese conducted several attacks against the army's left wing. In the sector held by the IX Corps, attacks estimated to be in regimental strength struck the ROK 9th Division. After intense fighting the South Koreans stopped these assaults and forced the enemy to withdraw. In the ROK Capital Division sector, two Chinese battalions tried to make a penetration. Although supported by large volumes of mortar and artillery fire, the Chinese were unable to drive the South Koreans from their positions and had to withdraw under punishing corps and division artillery fire.

The enemy's heaviest blow struck the U.S. I Corps. On the evening of 28 May five outpost positions of the U.S. 25th Division came under attack by an enemy regiment. These outposts, about 1,000 yards forward of the division's main line, guarded routes of approach to the division's center. Nicknamed Carson, Elko, Vegas, Berlin, and East Berlin, they were defended by platoons from the division's Turkish Brigade. Moving under extremely heavy artillery support, one Chinese battalion advanced on Carson and Elko. At the same time another enemy battalion, concealed by a smoke screen, attacked the center position, Vegas, while a third assaulted outposts Berlin and East Berlin on the right. Three hours after the attack began the enemy had reached the Turkish positions on Carson and Elko and were engaging the defenders in hand-to-hand combat. Unable to overcome the Turks the enemy withdrew, evidently to re-form, then attacked again. At outpost Elko, the action continued intermittently until midmorning of 29 May when the Chinese broke contact. A few minutes later they struck again at Elko. The fight continued about the outpost as the enemy pressed the attack. Finally, near midnight, the division ordered the outpost abandoned and the Turks withdrew to their main line of resistance.

Meanwhile, a furious fight had developed around outpost Vegas. One half hour after the Chinese began the attack on Vegas they reinforced their attacking elements with another battalion. Pushing forward through the artillery and mortar fire of both sides, they broke into the defensive positions and engaged the Turks in close combat. A Turkish company, rushed to reinforce the outpost, found hand-to-hand fights going on around the position. Two hours later the enemy began to break off the attack, once again suffering numerous casualties as the 25th Division artillery raked the enemy routes of withdrawal.

Just after daylight the Chinese attacked again with two battalions. This assault was also unsuccessful and the attackers withdrew. Two hours later the Turks counterattacked enemy elements on the north slope of the hill that contained outpost Vegas and drove them back. The Turks now had control of the entire outpost, but the Chinese seemed determined to seize Vegas at any cost. At midafternoon of the same day, 29 May, another battalion struck the battered position. The fight raged around the outpost for the remainder of the afternoon. Then at 2300, the order to withdraw came from division and the defenders fell back to their main line of resistance.

The enemy attack on outposts Berlin and East Berlin did not last long. After a bitter two-hour fire fight the enemy gave up the effort on these two positions and withdrew.

The Chinese had succeeded in occupying outposts Carson, Elko, and Vegas, but they paid a heavy price. The 25th Division reported evaluated enemy casualties in the battle as 2,200 killed and 1,057 wounded. In contrast the Turks reported their losses as 104 killed, 324 wounded, and 47 missing.

By the first of June it appeared certain to intelligence officers of the Eighth Army that the Chinese planned to strike a major blow soon. Their failure to follow up the May attacks against the U.S. I Corps indicated that those had been diversionary efforts to screen their real intentions. The continued movement and realignment of troops on the enemy front and rear and the large build-up of supplies near the battle zone further confirmed the army's belief that a large-scale Chinese attack impended. When the enemy blow would fall or where remained a matter of conjecture. As the first week of June passed the front remained relatively quiet. On the night of 10 June, the Chinese struck.

The enemy directed his efforts against the ROK II Corps, whose line bulged out to form a salient in the vicinity of Kumsong. Striking down both sides of the Pukhan River with two divisions the Chinese succeeded in forcing the right wing and center of the corps back about 4,000 yards in six days of heavy fighting. Not since the spring offensive of April–May 1951 had fighting on such a scale occurred.

The main enemy blow fell on the II Corps' right wing and center. Shortly after dark on 10 June a Chinese division attacked the right regiment of the ROK 5th Division, whose lines lay east of the Pukhan River. By seizing Hill 973, the dominant height in the regiment's sector, the enemy forced the South Koreans to fall back about 1,000 yards. Counterattacks by the reserve regiment of the 5th and a regiment from corps reserve the following morning failed to restore the main line of resistance or halt the enemy advance. The Chinese kept up their unrelenting pressure, forcing the 5th to withdraw again, and by 15 June the South Koreans had been pushed back to the east bank of the river at a point where the stream cut sharply eastward. There the division formed a new main line of resistance.

In the corps center the situation was just as critical. On the night of 12 June elements of another Chinese division struck the ROK 8th Division's right, which rested on the Pukhan. As the Chinese pressed forward they made several penetrations during the next twenty-four hours. Counterattacks by the reserve regiment of the 8th failed to halt the advance, and the Chinese began exploiting their gains. Attacking in regimental strength early on the morning of 14 June they soon enveloped the division's right regiment. The hard-pressed South Koreans began falling back under the weight of the enemy attack.

While the Chinese were attacking the II Corps' right, a smaller enemy force struck the ROK 20th Division, on the left of the X Corps. Evidently this was a holding attack, for the Chinese did not press their assault. But the collapse of the ROK 5th Division, on the II Corps' right, threatened the left of the X Corps. Lt. Gen. I. D. White, the X Corps commander, therefore narrowed the front of the 20th Division on 16 June and committed the ROK 7th Division, in corps reserve, on the left of the 20th to strengthen that flank. Other changes were being made to meet the situation in the ROK II Corps.

The failure of the 8th Division's right to hold coupled with the withdrawal of the 5th east of the river opened a gap between the divisions. The ROK II Corps commander filled this gap by committing the ROK 3d Division, in corps reserve, between the 8th and 5th Divisions on 15 June. At the same time General Taylor, in order to facilitate control, temporarily shifted the boundary between the II and X Corps westward to the river and gave the ROK 5th Division to the X Corps. To replace the ROK 3d, the army commander shifted the ROK 11th Division from the ROK I Corps over to the II Corps but kept it under army control.

The Chinese continued their attacks against the 8th Division, this time concentrating on the division's right and center. Under the heavy blows of the Chinese assault the South Koreans reeled back. A counterattack by elements of the division on 16 June failed to push the enemy back, and the 8th drew up on a new main line of resistance 3,000 yards south of the original one.

While the enemy concentrated his main effort against the ROK II Corps, he delivered several attacks on other parts of the front. Two outpost positions in front of the ROK 1st Division, in the U.S. I Corps, fell to the enemy near the end of June, after a prolonged attack by a Chinese regiment. Farther east, in the sector of the IX Corps, the Chinese employed forces in battalion and regimental strength in a thrust against the U.S. 3d and ROK 9th Divisions. They made minor penetrations in the lines of the 3d, but counterattacks quickly restored the positions. In the ROK 9th Division's sector the Chinese failed to make a dent. In the eastern sector of the Eighth Army's front, North Korean attacks forced a minor readjustment of main line of resistance positions on the X Corps' right wing. At the same time enemy forces were successful in seizing Hill 351, the northern anchor of the ROK I Corps line.

By 18 June, a slackening of enemy pressure enabled the corps to stabilize its front. General Taylor directed the commanders of the ROK II and U.S. X Corps to readjust their forces so as to permit the relief of the ROK 5th and 7th Divisions and to re-establish the boundary that existed between the corps before 15 June. The enemy made no further attacks on the II Corps front until the middle of July, just before the termination of hostilities.

Meanwhile a major airborne movement brought General Taylor additional troops from Japan. The 187th Airborne Regimental Combat Team assembled at two air bases in Japan on 21 June. In a matter of hours the entire unit, completely equipped for combat with vehicles, artillery, ammunition, and rations, was flown to forward air bases near the front. A few days later a similar movement took place. The 34th Regimental Combat Team (less one rifle battalion) of the 24th Division, similarly equipped, boarded aircraft at an air base near Tokyo and was flown to Pusan and Taegu.

Measured in terms of ground gained, the enemy attacks of mid-June on the ROK II Corps front were successful. The Chinese succeeded in pushing 15,000 yards of the corps front back about 4,000 yards. Moreover, their attacks caused three ROK divisions to be redeployed in reinforcing and counterattacking roles. Both sides incurred heavy casualties. The Chinese lost an estimated 6,628 men, and the II Corps reported 7,377 casualties as a direct result of the attacks.

Enemy attacks against the II Corps subsided after 18 June and by the end of the month action along the entire army front returned to routine patrolling and light attacks. But the army commander felt that the Chinese would again launch an attack in strength. It was not long in coming, this time against the left flank of the II Corps and the right flank of the IX Corps. The Capital Division, defending the IX Corps right-flank sector, faced northwest.

On the night of 13 July, the Chinese attacked the IX Corps' right flank with three divisions and soon broke through the South Korean lines. A good deal of confusion ensued as the Capital Division's right and center fell back. Some of the troops withdrew into the zone of the II Corps as units became entangled and lateral communication was lost. On the division's extreme left, things went somewhat better. There the units fell back in an orderly fashion under the crushing weight of Chinese attacks. But the collapse of the Capital Division made matters worse for the II Corps, whose situation was already serious.

The Chinese had timed their assault on the Capital Division with another attack, in division strength, against the ROK 6th Division, protecting the II Corps' left. After vainly trying to hold back the onslaught, the South Koreans began giving way. Their left flank was exposed by the withdrawal of the Capital Division, and the enemy was threatening to get into the rear of the 6th and cut it off. To prevent an enemy envelopment the division had no choice but to pull back. Retiring slowly, the 6th took a heavy toll of the attacking Chinese while farther to the east the ROK 8th and 3d Divisions moved back under heavy enemy pressure.

To meet the situation in the Eighth Army's center, General Taylor directed the commanders of the IX and II Corps to establish and hold a new main line of resistance along the south bank of the Kumsong River, a tributary of the Pukhan. In order to restore the line in the Capital Division zone, he permitted the U.S. 3d Division to be moved from its sector in the vicinity of Ch'orwon to the right wing of the IX Corps. The U.S. 2d Division extended its sector to the right to cover the position vacated by the 3d. The corps commander reinforced the 2d by attaching to it the 187th Airborne Regimental Combat Team, which dug in on the division's right. At the same time the 34th Regimental Combat Team (less one battalion) came up from Pusan and assumed the role of a counterattacking force. It took up positions in rear of the 2d Division.

In the II Corps the ROK 11th Division, in reserve, moved up to relieve the hard-pressed 6th. The ROK 7th Division on the left wing of X Corps moved out of the line, and its place was taken by the U.S. 45th Division. The 7th then came over to the II Corps. Further changes occurred in the corps when the ROK 6th hastily reorganized and moved into the sectors held by the ROK 3d and 5th Divisions. The two latter divisions went into corps reserve. After this reorganization the II Corps counterattacked on 17 July with three divisions in an attempt to seize the high ground along the Kumsong and establish a new main line of resistance. By 20 July the II Corps attained its objective and held it. No attempt was made to restore the original line, inasmuch as the imminence of an armistice made it tactically unnecessary to expend lives for terrain not essential to the security of the Eighth Army's front.

Enemy losses in July were tremendous. The army estimated that the Chinese lost over 72,000 men, more than 25,000 of them killed. Out of the five Chinese armies that had been identified in the attacks upon the II and IX Corps, the enemy had lost the equivalent of seven divisions.

While the fighting raged on the central front the negotiators at Panmunjom rapidly approached an agreement on armistice terms. On 19 July agreement was reached on all points by both sides. The next day liaison and staff officers began the task of drawing up the boundaries of the demilitarized zone. All details of the armistice agreement and its implementation were completed in a week. At 1000 hours on 27 July Lt. Gen. William K. Harrison, Jr., the senior United Nations delegate to the armistice negotiations, signed the armistice papers. At the same time the senior enemy delegate, General Nam Il, placed his signature on the documents. The signing took place at this time to permit the armistice to go into effect at 2200 hours of the same day, as required by the agreement. Later General Clark, for the United Nations, General Kim Il Sung, for North Korea, and General Peng Teh-Huai, for the Chinese forces on the peninsula, affixed their signatures.

The conflict in Korea had lasted three years, one month, and two days. It had destroyed Korean homes, fields, and factories, wrecked the nation's economy, and threatened the populace with famine and disease. It had consumed the lives of hundreds of thousands of civilians and soldiers from nations all over the face of the globe. Many had died who a short time before had known Korea only as an exotic place name on a map. The signing of the armistice brought an end to the shooting; it did not bring an end to the ideological war. "We have won an armistice on a single battleground," said President Eisenhower as the Panmunjom negotiators reached agreement, "not peace in the world. We may not now relax our guard nor cease our quest."

Despite the failure to settle the issue in Korea, the United States and its partners in the fight against aggression had gained some insight into the manner of foe that opposed them. They learned that the communist adversary would use every means at his command to gain an advantage, both political and military; that he was willing, as in his use of human-sea tactics, to expend his soldiers' lives prodigally in order to offset superior fire power. And, most important, they learned that the enemy, though powerful, was not invulnerable.

The countries that fought under the flag of the United Nations to prevent the conquest of South Korea had demonstrated their ability to put aside differences and act in concert against a common enemy. That nations of highly diverse cultural, religious, and racial background were willing to place their forces under a single command, in this case the United States, was evidence that free men could rise above national pride in their never-ending fight to remain free.

SECTION 8

1 July–31 December 1952

Bird's-Eye View of Capital Hill, dominated by enemy terrain, background.

Treating a ROK Soldier wounded on Capital Hill, 8 September, right.

QUAD .50's adding fire power to a counterattack on Old Baldy, 21 September.

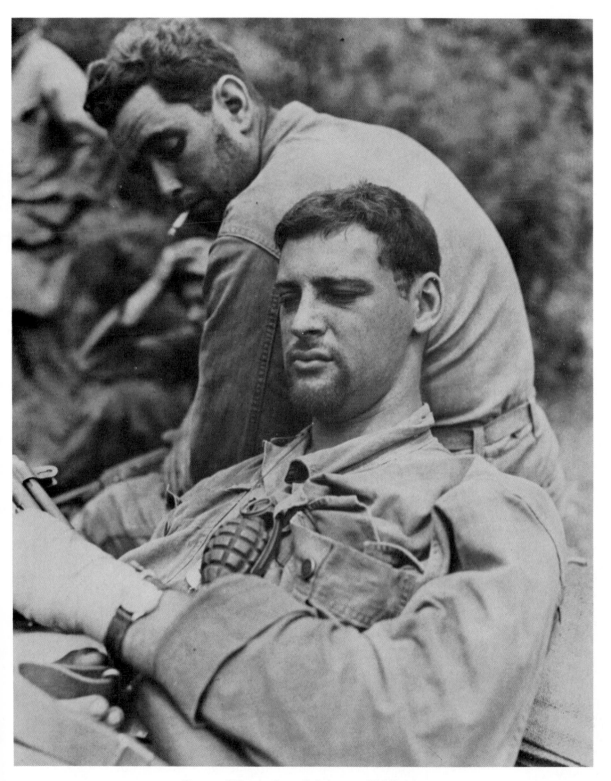

BATTLE WEARY from fighting on Old Baldy.

ROK MP's Trying To Get Warm near White Horse, 8 October.

WHITE HORSE (Hill 395), one of two key heights northwest of Ch'orwon attacked by enemy units in October. Vehicle is a 90-mm. gun motor carriage M36.

ASSEMBLY POINT for ROK 9th Division infantrymen.

Wounded on White Horse, two ROK 9th Division soldiers head for medical treatment.

MEDICAL AID MEN DRESSING WOUNDS at an aid station near base of White Horse.

F-86 SABREJETS OVER NORTH KOREA hunting for MIG-15's. During September pilots from the Fifth Air Force shot down sixty-four MIG's at a cost of seven Sabrejets.

ADJUSTING ROCKETS on the wing of an AD Sky-raider before the take-off.

BANSHEES returning to the USS *Kearsarge* after a mission over Korea.

WINTER, 1952

T66 MULTIPLE ROCKET LAUNCHERS in action, 40th Division sector, 26 November. Except for brief encounters with the enemy, most of the front remained relatively quiet during November and December.

PRESIDENT-ELECT DWIGHT D. EISENHOWER in Korea, December 1952. Above, the President-elect is with Maj. Gen. James C. Fry, Commanding General, 2d Division. Left page above, he has dinner with 3d Division troops, south of Ch'orwon. Below, he leaves 3d Division area by jeep; in back seat are Lt. Gen. Reuben E. Jenkins, Commanding General, IX Corps (left), and Maj. Gen. George W. Smythe, Commanding General, 3d Division.

SECTION 9

1 January–27 July 1953

CLEANING SNOW OFF THE FLIGHT DECK of an aircraft carrier.

TROOPS FROM THAILAND arriving at Inch'on, January 1953.

DESTINATION KOJE-DO. Troops from the 23d Infantry, scheduled for guard duty at the prisoner compound, board ship via cargo net.

PHILIPPINE SOLDIERS attached to the 45th Division put on snow suits before leaving on a night patrol mission, north of Yanggu.

INSIDE A BUNKER on Hill 200.

LUNCH PICNIC-STYLE. The men are from Company K, 15th Infantry.

NAVY MEN WORKING IN A SNOWSTORM at an emergency airfield.

PATROL OF THE 35TH INFANTRY studying a map of enemy terrain. Armored vests are clearly visible on the two men at left.

ENTERTAINMENT for 55th Transportation Truck Battalion, Eighth Army. The cast is from the motion picture, "The Girls of Pleasure Island."

TROOPS BOARDING A HELICOPTER to be airlifted up to the line.

ENEMY TERRAIN as seen through chicken wire in front of an outpost. The wire helped to keep grenades from coming into the bunkers; often the wire was used as a base for supporting camouflage material.

GENERAL MARK W. CLARK, Commander in Chief, U.N. Command (right), at the Greek Battalion headquarters. With him are (from left) Lt. Gen. Reuben E. Jenkins, Commanding General, IX Corps; Lt. Gen. Maxwell D. Taylor, Commanding General, Eighth Army; and Lt. Col. George Koumanacos, Commanding Officer of the Greek Battalion.

WOUNDED 7TH DIVISION INFANTRYMAN is rushed away from the fight on Pork Chop Hill.

"He's the best grenade thrower in the company."

CARTING AWAY TWO CHINESE PRISONERS captured on Pork Chop Hill, 17 April 1953.

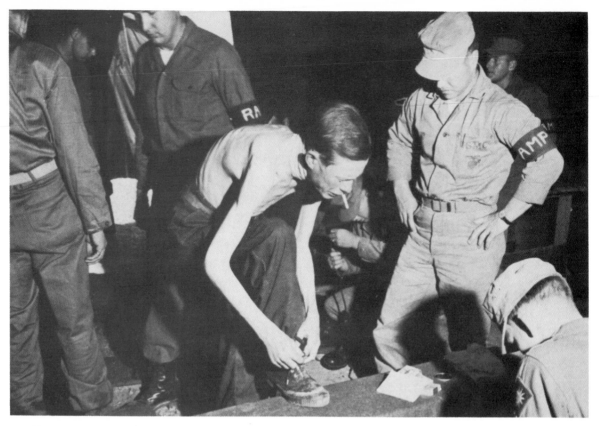

EMACIATED AND WOUNDED AMERICAN receiving new clothing at Freedom Village, Panmunjom.

U.N. AND NORTH KOREAN OFFICERS acknowledging receipt of returnees.

LIBERATED AMERICANS are escorted down the ramp of a C-124 upon arrival in Japan for medical treatment before continuing the trip back to the United States.

Operation LITTLE SWITCH, April 1953. On 11 April agreement was reached for the exchange of 605 U.N. prisoners for 6,030 enemy prisoners.

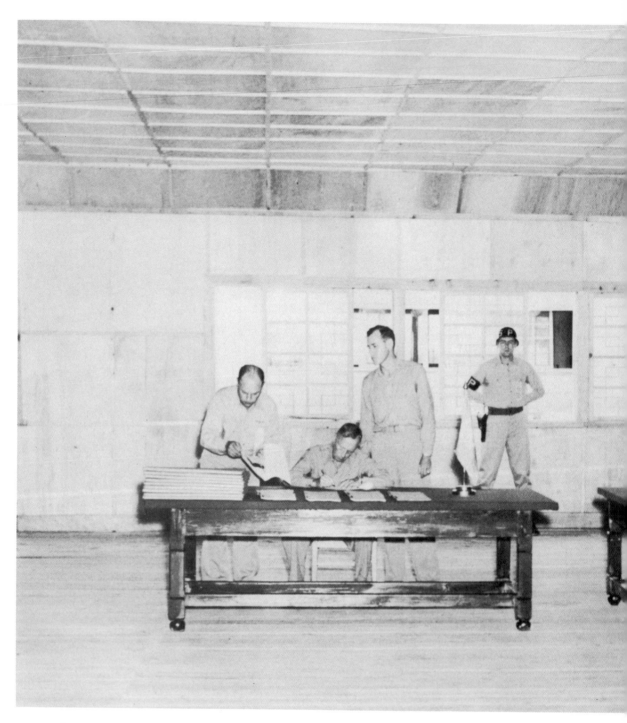

SIGNING THE ARMISTICE AGREEMENT at 1000 hours, 27 July 1953, Panmunjom. Lt. Gen. William K.

Harrison, Jr., signs for the United Nations (left), and General Nam Il for the Communists (right).

7th Division Position just before it was abandoned, 31 July.

40TH DIVISION TROOPS all packed and ready to leave Heartbreak Ridge.

1ST MARINE DIVISION MEN after receiving word of the armistice.

First Shipment of Repatriated Men from Korea docking at San Francisco, 23 August.

Maj. Gen. William F. Dean boarding a plane at Tokyo for home, 21 September.

List of Pictorial Sources

The following list gives the origin of all photographs and cartoons which appear in this book. The photographs were selected from those in the files of the Army Signal Corps (SC), the Air Force (USAF), the Navy (USN), and the Marine Corps (USMC). The cartoons were published originally in the Pacific Edition of the Army newspaper, *Stars and Stripes*. Further information concerning photographs may be secured from the agency of origin, Washington 25, D. C. Inquiries should include the number of the photograph.

Page	Source	Number	Page	Source	Number
31	USAF	79347 AC	54 (bottom)	SC	356897
32–33	SC	355931	55 (top)	SC	357169
34	SC	355593	55 (bottom)	SC	357402
35	SC	355566	56 (top)	SC	362393
36–37 (top)	SC	355553	56 (bottom)	SC	362139
36 (bottom)	USN	425403	56–57 (center)	USAF	78972 AC
37 (bottom)	USN	425473	57 (top)	SC	356733
38 (top)	SC	355563	57 (bottom)	SC	356880
38 (bottom)	SC	355565	58	SC	361469
39 (top)	SC	355547	59	*Stars and Stripes*	(cartoon)
39 (bottom)	SC	356269	60 (top)	SC	357386
40 (top)	SC	355576	60 (bottom)	SC	357227
41 (top)	SC	355574	61 (top)	SC	357742
40–41 (bottom)	SC	356475	61 (bottom)	SC	357320
42	SC	356295	62–63	SC	358042
43	SC	356682	64 (top)	SC	358094
44 (top)	SC	356636	64 (bottom)	SC	358093
44 (bottom)	SC	356696	65	*Stars and Stripes*	(cartoon)
45 (top)	SC	356347	66–67	USAF	unknown
45 (bottom)	SC	356713	68 (top)	SC	358336
46 (top left)	SC	355939	68 (bottom)	SC	358494
46 (top right)	SC	355940	69	SC	358774
46 (bottom)	SC	356671	70 (left)	SC	359414
47	SC	356736	70 (right)	SC	358263
48	SC	375189	71	SC	358159
49	*Stars and Stripes*	(cartoon)	72	SC	358508
53	SC	FEC–51–4601	73 (top)	SC	358624
54 (top)	SC	356902	73 (bottom)	SC	358622

Page	Source	Number	Page	Source	Number
74–75 (top)	USN	426777	134 (top)	SC	367550
74–75 (bottom)	USN	426781	134 (bottom)	SC	368661
76–77	SC	359744	135	SC	368660
77	SC	359404	136 (top)	SC	368676
80–81 (top)	SC	359910	136 (bottom)	SC	368540
80–81 (bottom)	SC	359805	137 (top)	SC	368543
82	SC	360254	137 (bottom)	SC	369065
83 (top)	SC	360255	138 (top)	SC	368815
83 (bottom)	SC	362325	138 (bottom)	SC	369479
84–85	SC	361405	139 (top)	SC	368813
85	USAF	79951 AC	139 (bottom)	SC	368690
86	SC	362092	140 (top)	SC	369492
87 (top)	SC	362126	140 (bottom)	SC	369216
87 (bottom)	SC	362114	141	SC	368735
88 (top)	USAF	79676 AC	142 (top)	USN	429640
88 (bottom)	USAF	79638 AC	142 (bottom)	SC	368949
89	USAF	79628 AC	143 (top)	SC	369402
90	SC	361980	143 (bottom)	SC	370299
90–91	SC	362117	144	USN	429680
92	USMC	A–8613	145 (top)	USN	429857
93	USMC	A–7091	145 (bottom)	USN	429641
94	USMC	A–8941	146	USN	430064
95	USMC	A–8759	147	USN	430052
96	USAF	79649 AC	148 (top)	USN	429644
97	USAF	80332 AC	148 (bottom)	USN	429685
98–99	USN	708178	149	USN	429504
121	USMC	A–7797	150 (top)	USMC	A–8615–A
122 (top)	SC	365854	150 (bottom)	SC	369995
122 (middle)	SC	365440	151	SC	369801
122 (bottom)	SC	365791	152 (top)	Stars and Stripes	(cartoon)
123 (top)	SC	365849	152 (bottom)	USAF	80508 AC
123 (middle)	SC	365755	153 (top)	USAF	79848 AC
123 (bottom)	SC	365760	153 (bottom)	USAF	79852 AC
124 (top left)	SC	365542	157	USN	428390
124 (top right)	SC	365570	158	SC	373296
124 (bottom)	SC	365544	158–59	SC	372740
125 (top left)	SC	365547	160	SC	373647
125 (top right)	SC	FEC–51–23765	161 (top)	SC	372280
125 (bottom)	SC	365537	161 (bottom)	SC	374102
126	USN	428635	162	SC	374889
127 (top)	USN	428637	163 (top)	USAF	80703 AC
127 (bottom)	USN	428678	163 (bottom)	SC	375088
128 (left)	USAF	79842 AC	164 (top)	SC	FEC–51–26651
128 (right)	USAF	A–79842 AC	164 (bottom)	SC	376086
129	USAF	80333 AC	165	SC	376744
132	SC	368493	166	SC	376719
133 (top)	SC	368504	167 (top)	SC	FEC–51–27649
133 (bottom)	USMC	A–156986	167 (bottom)	SC	376599

Page	Source	Number	Page	Source	Number
255 (top)	SC	421635	298	USN	449917
255 (bottom)	SC	405834	299 (top)	SC	411730
256	SC	390177	299 (bottom)	SC	411732
257 (top)	SC	390612	300 (top)	SC	416354
257 (bottom)	SC	390129	300 (bottom)	SC	416389
258–59	SC	392504	301	SC	412361
260 (top)	SC	399346	305	SC	416204
260 (bottom)	SC	395043	306 (top)	USN	478280
261 (top)	SC	397517	306 (bottom)	SC	426136
261 (bottom)	SC	398702	307	SC	416243
262 (top)	USAF	83054 AC	308 (top)	SC	424253
262 (bottom)	USN	444157	308 (bottom)	SC	422625
263	USAF	81504 AC	309	SC	415948
264 (top)	Stars and Stripes	(cartoon)	310 (top)	USN	480136
264 (bottom)	SC	406096	310 (bottom)	SC	419512
265	SC	406069	311	SC	FEC–53–2238
266	USN	443864	312 (top)	SC	422077
286–87	SC	423081	312 (bottom)	SC	424400
288	SC	407539	313	SC	428313
289	SC	426124	314	SC	422963
290 (top)	Stars and Stripes	(cartoon)	315 (top)	Stars and Stripes	(cartoon)
290 (bottom)	SC	408532	315 (bottom)	SC	422968
291	SC	404701	316 (top)	USN	633215
292–93	SC	418366	316 (bottom)	USN	481024
292 (bottom)	SC	418372	317	USAF	82929 AC
293 (bottom)	SC	418362	318–19	USN	625914
294	SC	418375	320	SC	431799
295	SC	418380	321 (top)	SC	432931
296	USAF	82042 AC	321 (bottom)	USN	626455
297 (top)	USN	448324	322	SC	425766
297 (bottom)	USN	480057	323	SC	435044

☆ U.S. GOVERNMENT PRINTING OFFICE : 1982 O – 365–480 :